Nuggets
of History

For The
Slightly Interested

or

Easily Bored!
In Small Doses
Compiled & Edited
by

Thomas J. Morrow

Cover Design By Helen Hartley

ISBN: ISBN-13:978-1519117496
ISBN-10:1519117493

Table of Contents

AUTHOR'S NOTE..viii

1 THE PRINTED WORD...11

2 THE ADAMS BOYS..12

3 LIGHT-HORSE HARRY LEE OF VIRGINIA............................15

4 BENEDICT ARNOLD:TRAITOR TO THE REVOLUTION...........18

5 THE 'HERO OF THE TWO WORLDS'......................................21

6 AARON BURR: A FORGOTTEN MAN.....................................24

7 AMERICA'S FIRST SPY NETWORK..27

8 'THE FOX' HAD THE BRITISH ON THE RUN...........................30

9 THE WHOLE SHEBANG, LOCK, STOCK & BARREL................33

10 THE FOUNDING OF MISSION SAN LUIS REY......................36

11 THE RISE AND FALL OF NAPOLEON BONAPARTE..............39

IT'S OUR MANIFEST DESTINY..42

12 THE BUYING OF OUR HEARTLAND....................................42

13 JOHN C. FREMONT:...45

PATHFINDER TO THE WEST..45

14 LAFITTE: THE SCOUNDREL OR HERO?.............................48

15 DOLLEY MADISON:..50

FIRST HOSTESS OF THE UNITED STATES................................50

16 THE BLACK HAWK WAR..53

17 THE IOWA-MISSOURI HONEY WAR..................................56

18 'OLD HICTORY' – A NOT SO NICE MAN 59

19 THE GADSDEN PURCHASE...62

20 CAVE COUTS PIONEER OF SAN DIEGO'S NORTH COUNTY................65

21 THE GREAT POTATO FAMINE 68

22 THE SURVEY LINE THAT MARKS FOUR.............................70

U.S. STATES..70

23 ROBERT E. LEE: HERO OF THE SOUTH............................73

24 ULYSSES S. GRANT..76

HERO OF THE CIVIL WAR..76

25 THE SHORTEST TERM U.S. PRESIDENT............................79

26 CRAZY HORSE: THE NOBLE, DEFIANT NATIVE AMERICAN................82

27 HARVARD DIDN'T WANT THEIR MONEY...........................85

28 THE NEARLY FORGOTTEN PRESIDENT.............................88

29 JESSE JAMES: ROBIN HOOD, ROGUE,...............................91

OR VICIOUS KILLER?...91

HISTORY'S BUSIEST CENTURY..94

30 THE GREAT WAR: CLASH OF THE VICTORIAN COUSINS................94

31 THE SAGA OF THE FORD FAMILY..................................97

32 THE 'REAL' FATHER OF MODERN ELECTRICITY.................................100

33 JOSEPH PULITZER: MAN BEHIND THE 'PRIZES'............................103

34 HEARST: FATHER OF 'YELLOW JOURNALISM'..............................106

35 THE CURMUDGEON OF...109

THE AMERICAN PRESS..109

36 'LUCKY LINDY' – 'THE LONE EAGLE'.......................................112

37 THE FATHER OF THE AMERICAN..115

AIR FORCE..115

38 AMERICA'S 1ST FLYING ACE: EDDIE RICKENBACKER.....................118

39 THE GREAT SAGE OF MIDDLE AMERICA.....................................121

40 ONE OF OUR WORST PRESIDENTS..124

41 THE OWENS VALLEY WAR...127

42 THE TEAPOT DOME SCANDAL...130

43 1939: IT'S STILL THE BEST MOVIE YEAR....................................133

44 A SELF-MADE IOWA BOY...135

45 THEY LED US INTO AND OUT OF THE GREAT DEPRESSION.............138

46 WHY HITLER SNUBBED THE AMERICAN BUND............................150

47 THE SPY WHO PLAYED PRO BASEBALL......................................153

48 'THE BATTLING BASTARDS OF BATAAN'....................................156

49 THE BATAAN DEATH MARCH...159

50 THE COOK WHO WAS AN UNLIKELY HERO.................................162

51 AN UNBELIEVABLE EFFORT OF PRODUCTION...................164

52 THE "WILD" FATHER OF U.S. INTELLIGENCE.....................167

53 THE 'WORLD'S MOST BEAUTIFUL INVENTOR'..................170

54 RATIONING DURING WORLD WAR II...............................173

55 AMERICA'S REAL HERO MOVIE STAR...............................176

56 FIELD MARSHAL ROMMEL:...179

THE DESERT FOX...179

57 THE DEADLY SKIES OVER EUROPE 182

58 THE PORT CHICAGO...191

DISASTER & MUTINY..191

59 A MOST DANGEROUS MAN..194

60 THE BATTLE OF THE BULGE...197

61 THE MALMEDY MASSACRE..200

62 THE GENERAL BEHIND THE GENERALS...........................203

63 PATTON: AN AMERICAN FOLK HERO..............................206

64 EDDIE ALBERT – AN UNSUNG HERO...............................208

65 THE MAN WHO WOULD BE BOND.................................211

66 30-ASSAULT UNIT...215

67 HARRY S. TRUMAN: 'HIS ACCIDENTCY'...........................218

68 WHEN 'FATHER' WAS IN..221

WASHINGTON, D.C..221

69 THE ROSENBERG: SPIES..224

OR POLITICAL DUPES?..224

70 THE FOUNDING OF AMERICA'S NEW PASTIME..............................227

ABOUT THE AUTHOR...230

AUTHOR'S NOTE

This book is designed to interest more people, especially young students, in the history of our country and the world.

Show me a person who is or was bored with history and I'll show you someone who had a boring history teacher. Some of the greatest stories known are taken from history.

Unless you lived it, history is left to interpretation. Even witnesses have different first-person views of events they've experienced. The further back in time, the more history is open interpretation. The information in this book was compiled from a variety of sources, including autobiographies and biographies of many of the individuals listed. A great deal of the historical events is listed from Internet sources, including Wikipedia, which provides valuable, ready sources of in-depth historical data gathered from a vast number of essayists, historians, and educators. And, because of Wikipedia's many sources, a number of scholars and history buffs have challenged various interpretations and stated facts. The Bible is a good example of historical interpretation.

The important point to remember when studying history is its importance to humanity. History does repeat itself. That being true, how can we know where we're going if we don't know where we've been?

This book offers "thumb-nail" sketches of notable individuals and events that have been important to our history. Each mini-essay is but a layer of historical information, which is designed to be peeled back to reveal more information and events for expanded study. The first essay about the Magna Carta refers to King John, his brother Richard, Pope Innocent III, Edward I, and Henry III, each with an intriguing biography of their own, which opens up at least five more great stories of history.

So, for those of you who are only slightly interested in history, this book should whet your appetite for some interesting, and often, fascinating stories in history. Show me a person who is, or was, bored with history and I will show you someone who had a boring history teacher. Some of the greatest stories known are taken from history.

Enjoy, *Tom Morrow*

IN THE BEGINNING

1 THE PRINTED WORD

Regardless of your religious beliefs or philosophy, the first printings of the Bible was the catalyst for spurring wide-spread education and literacy, bringing the nations of the world closer together.

Printing with movable type can be traced back to 1040 AD, invented by a Chinaman, **Bi Sheng**, who began using movable wood blocks to print. In 1392, the Koreans were using movable copper type to print. But the dawn of modern-day typesetting began in the mid-1400 by **Johannes Gutenberg** of Mainz, Germany.

Unlike his Oriental counterparts, Gutenberg's process made printing practical, which led to a revolution in mass communications. Until the advancements of the computer, Gutenberg' method remained the principal way to print until the late 20th century.

Gutenberg's method centered around the key innovation involving the making of a punch-stamped mold that could cast large amount of metal type with precision for a new kind of press using oil-based ink. His first printing job for mass distribution was 180 copies of the Bible in 1455. Until that time, the Bible was painstakingly done by hand by clergymen, taking as long as 20 years just to produce on volume. That first Gutenberg edition was printed in Latin.

His technology spread throughout Europe and by 1520, more than 200 different editions of the Bible had been produced. While Gutenberg printed his first volumes in Latin, printers began producing other books, posters, simple news announcements in their native languages, which made books on all subjects readily available to not just scholars, but to the general population. This resulted in people becoming more literate. News and ideas spread quickly and widely, bringing the world closer together.

Gutenberg never profited from his invention. In fact, it caused him to end up bankrupt. While under development, he had financial problems, and to make matters worse, his financial backer, **Johann Fust**, became impatient and successfully sued Gutenberg, forcing him to relinquish all claims to his printing process. Fust went on to make a fortune from Bible sales. Gutenberg died in 1468 broke and in relative obscurity.

2 THE ADAMS BOYS

Sam and John Adams were a "one-two" punch in the winning of independence from Great Britain. The two were cousins, but could not be more different in personality and methodology – only their goal was identical.

Samuel Adams was born Sept. 27, 1722, in Boston. He was a brewer among other trades, none very successful. Sam spent more time fighting and rebelling against the crushing taxes levied by the British, making him one of the key figures of the American Revolution.

Sam's cousin, John Adams, was an attorney who became one of the most important American statesman, diplomat, and a leading advocate of independence from Great Britain. Sam and John joined John Hancock as Massachusetts delegates to the Continental Congress and were the driving force in getting independence declared from Great Britain.

Well-educated, John Adams was a political theorist who promoted republicanism as well as a strong central government. John wrote prolifically about his ideas -- both in published works and in letters to his wife and key adviser Abigail Adams.

But John wasn't as quick to embrace the Revolution as was his cousin. In the early days of the Revolution, John was uneasy about the radical views and actions of Sam and questioned whether the colonists could win.

Sam was brought up in a religious and politically-active family. A graduate of Harvard College, he was unsuccessful in business and tax collector before concentrating on politics. As an influential official of the Massachusetts House of Representatives and the Boston Town Meeting in the 1760s, Adams was a part of a movement opposed to the British Parliament's efforts to tax the colonists without their consent.

His 1768 pamphlet calling for non-cooperation prompted the occupation of Boston by British soldiers. This caused the Boston Massacre of 1770. Ironically, it was Cousin John who defended the six British soldiers accused of gunning down Bostonians on a town street. John provided a principled, controversial, and successful legal defense of the accused British soldiers, because he believed in the right to counsel and the "protection of innocence."

Although angered by John's defense of the British soldiers, Sam rightly pointed out everyone is entitled to a fair trial, regardless of who they are.

Sam was the ringleader of the so-called "Tea Party" raid on a British ship. While Sam was in on the planning, it remains unclear as to his participation in tossing tea into Boston Harbor.

John was a political theorist who promoted republicanism and a strong central government. He wrote prolifically both in published works and in letters to his wife and key adviser Abigail Adams.

In 1776, John assisted Thomas Jefferson in drafting the Declaration of Independence. A political theorist and historian, John largely wrote the Massachusetts Constitution in 1780; he nominated George Washington to be commander-in-chief, and helped write the U.S. Constitution. John became George Washington's vice president and later the second U.S. President.

Historians have praised Sam Adams for steering his fellow colonists towards independence long before the outbreak of the <u>Revolutionary War</u>. This view gave way to negative assessments of Sam. He was portrayed as a master of <u>propaganda</u> who provoked <u>mob violence</u> to achieve his goals. Some modern scholars argue these traditional depictions are myths contradicted by the historical record.

There's little doubt the Revolutionary War, the Declaration of Independence, and the U.S. Constitution wouldn't have successfully occurred when they did without the Adams boys. John's revolutionary credentials secured him two terms as George Washington's vice president, and his own election in 1796 as the second president. During his one term as president, he encountered ferocious attacks by the Jeffersonian Republicans, as well as the dominant faction in his own Federalist Party led by his bitter enemy Alexander Hamilton.

In 1800, John Adams was defeated for re-election by Thomas Jefferson and retired to Massachusetts. He later resumed his friendship with Jefferson. He and his wife founded an accomplished family line of politicians, diplomats, and historians now referred to as the Adams political family. Adams was the father of John Quincy Adams, the sixth President of the United States. His achievements have received greater recognition in modern times, though his contributions were not initially as celebrated as those of other Founders. Adams was the first U.S. president to reside in the executive mansion that eventually became known as the White House.

3 LIGHT-HORSE HARRY LEE OF VIRGINIA

Henry Lee III (1756 -- 1818), and his son, Robert E. Lee (1809-1870) were two of America's greatest military generals, both serving in rebel armies.

Henry Lee, affectionately known as "Light-Horse" Harry Lee, started out as a captain in the cavalry of the Continental Army during the Revolutionary War when the 13 colonies "rebelled" against Great Britain.

Robert E. Lee rose to the rank of colonel in the Union Army and was superintendent at West Point when the Civil War broke out. President Lincoln offered him a high leadership position the Union Army, but Robert E. resigned his U.S. commission after 32 years of service, and returned to his native Virginia, becoming a rebel Confederate general in the Army of Northern Virginia.

"Light Horse" Harry had an illustration career, not only during the Revolutionary War, but in politics as Governor of Virginia and later as the Virginia Representative to the United States Congress.

But it's Harry's son, Robert, who has gone down in history books as one of the most popular of American generals, leading the Confederate Army to multiple victories even though he often was out-manned, out-gunned, and woefully under-equipped.

Harry was the second cousin of Richard Henry Lee, one of the signers of the Declaration of Independence.

Upon graduating from college (which is now Princeton University), Harry became an attorney, but when the Revolutionary War began, he joined the Virginia dragoons as a captain, attached to the 1st Division of the Continental Light Horse cavalry.

In 1778, Lee was promoted from captain to major and given command of a mixed corps of cavalry and infantry. His agile horsemanship in battle earned him the nickname of "Light Horse" Harry. Much to the chagrin of the British, his dragoons and infantry would attack with "hit and run" guerilla tactics. His troops became known as "Lee's Legion."

For his battle successes, the Congress awarded Harry a "gold medal," an honor given only to officers of general rank. Then Harry was promoted to lieutenant colonel and sent to South Carolina where they joined up with "The Swamp Fox," Francis Marion.

Harry was present at Yorktown when British General Cornwallis surrendered to George Washington. Harry ended his military career in 1781 as a major general. He left the Army to serve in state and federal government.

When George Washington died in 1799, Harry eulogized the nation's first President at his funeral attended by 4,000 mourners.

Harry fell upon hard financial times during the Panic of 1796–1797 and served one year in debtors' prison when his son, Robert E., was only two years old.

Later, during a brawl, Harry suffered internal injuries as well as head and face wounds. He sailed to the West Indies in an effort to recuperate from his injuries. "Light Horse" Harry Lee died on March 25, 1818, on Cumberland Island, off the coast of Georgia where he was buried with full military honors. In 1913, Harry's remains were moved to the Lee family crypt on the campus of Washington & Lee University in Lexington, Virginia.

History has more or less forgotten "Light Horse" Harry Lee, but he was briefly remembered with the fictional character of "Colonel Burwell" in the recent Mel Gibson film, "The Patriot." The Burwell character is believed to have been inspired by the Revolutionary War exploits of "Light Horse" Harry Lee.

4 BENEDICT ARNOLD:TRAITOR TO THE REVOLUTION

Most Americans have heard the name "Benedict Arnold," usually in a disparaging manner. He was a businessman turned Continental Army officer, serving in America's Revolutionary War.

The problem was he jumped ships to join the British.

Arnold originally fought with distinction and valor for the Continental Army, but when he thought he was being unfairly mistreated as a hero of the Revolution, he defected to the British Army.

Born in Connecticut, Arnold was a merchant operating ships on the Atlantic Ocean when the war broke out in 1775. After joining the Army, he was commissioned a captain and rose through the ranks as he distinguished himself through acts of intelligence and valor. Arnold's actions included leadership and bravery in the battles at Montreal and Quebec. Also during the capture of Fort Ticonderoga in 1775

He was promoted to major general and participated in operations and action during the pivotal Battles of Saratoga in

1777.

Despite Arnold's successes, he was passed over for promotion by the Continental Congress while other officers claimed credit for some of his accomplishments. Adversaries in military and political circles brought charges of corruption or other malfeasance, but most often he was acquitted in formal inquiries. Congress investigated his accounts and found the colonists owed Arnold a lot of money because he spent much of his own money on the war effort.

Frustrated and bitter at this, as well the alliance with France and failure of Congress to accept Britain's 1778 proposal to grant full self-governance in the colonies, Arnold decided to change sides and opened secret negotiations with the British.

In July 1780, he was offered, continued to pursue, and was awarded command of West Point (then a Continental Army fortress guarding the Hudson River). Arnold's scheme to surrender the fort to the British was exposed when American forces captured British Major John André, who was carrying papers that revealed the plot.

Upon learning of André's capture, Arnold fled down the Hudson River to a British ship, narrowly avoiding capture by the forces of George Washington, who had been alerted to the plot.

Arnold received a commission as a brigadier general in the British Army, an annual pension of £360, and a lump sum of over £6,000. He led British forces on raids in Virginia, and against New London and Groton, Connecticut, before the war effectively ended with the American victory at Yorktown.

In the winter of 1782, Arnold moved to London with his second wife, Margaret Shippen Arnold. He was well-received by King George III and the Tories, but frowned upon by the Whigs. In 1787, he returned to the merchant business with his sons Richard and Henry in St. John, New Brunswick. He returned to London to settle permanently in 1791, where he died in 1801.

Because of the way he changed sides, his name quickly became a byword in the United States for treason or betrayal. His conflicting legacy is recalled in the ambiguous nature of some of the memorials that have been placed in his honor.

5 THE 'HERO OF THE TWO WORLDS'

There is one Frenchman whose name will live forever in historic revolutionary endeavors – the Marquis de Lafayette.

Gilbert du Motier, Marquis de Lafayette, was born Sept. 6, 1757. He was one of the outstanding figures of both American and French revolutions. Here in the U.S., he was known simply as *"Lafayette."*

Lafayette was a French aristocrat and military officer who became a close friend of George Washington, Alexander Hamilton, and Thomas Jefferson. He came from a wealthy family; was commissioned an officer at age 13, and was convinced the American revolutionary cause was noble. He traveled to the New World where the Continental Congress made the 19-year-old a major general, though initially he was not given troops to command.

After Lafayette offered to serve without pay, Congress commissioned him a major general. Among Lafayette's early advocates included Benjamin Franklin, who urged Congress to accommodate the young Frenchman.

General George Washington, Commander In Chief of the Continental Army, met Lafayette at a dinner in 1777. Washington took Lafayette to his military camp and made the young Frenchman a member of his staff.

Congress regarded Lafayette's general officer commission as "honorary," while he considered himself a full-fledged commander. Washington told Lafayette a command because of his foreign birth, but the young French officer distinguished himself battle after battle. Wounded during the Battle of Brandywine, Lafayette still managed to organize an orderly retreat. He served with distinction in the Battle of Rhode Island.

In the middle of the Revolutionary War, Lafayette returned to France to lobby for an increase in French support, which ultimately gave victory to the Americans over the British. He sailed back to America in 1780, and was given senior positions in Washington's Continental Army.

In 1781, American troops under Lafayette's command blocked British forces until other American and French forces could position themselves for the decisive Siege of Yorktown, Virginia, resulting in Lord Cornwallis' surrender, which ended the war.

Lafayette returned to France and, in 1787, and was appointed to the Assembly of Notables. He helped write the French Declaration of the Rights of Man and of the Citizen, with the assistance of Thomas Jefferson. He became a member of the Chamber of Deputies, a position he held for the remainder of his life.

After leading the citizens to storm the Bastille (prison) during the French Revolution, Lafayette was appointed Commander-In-Chief of the French National Guard, and tried to steer a moderate course, but radical factions ordered his arrest and spent more than five years in prison. When Bonaparte Napoleon came to power as Emperor of France, he ordered Lafayette's release.

On June 22, 1815, four days after the Battle of Waterloo, Napoleon abdicated as French Emperor. Lafayette tried to save him by arranging for Napoleon's passage to America where the former emperor could live in exile, but the British prevented that from happening. The man who nearly conquered all of Europe would be held prisoner by the British on the small island of Saint Helena in the south Atlantic for the rest of his life.

The Marquis de Lafayette died on May 20, 1834, at the age of 76. He is buried in Picpus Cemetery in Paris under soil from Boston's Bunker Hill. For his accomplishments in the service of both France and the United States, he is sometimes known as "The Hero of the Two Worlds."

In the United States, President Andrew Jackson ordered that Lafayette receive the same memorial honors bestowed on Washington in 1799. Both Houses of Congress were draped in black bunting for 30 days, and members wore mourning badges. Congress urged Americans to follow similar mourning practices. Later in 1834, former President John Quincy Adams gave a eulogy of Lafayette that lasted three hours, calling him "high on the list of the pure and disinterested benefactors of mankind."

6 AARON BURR: A FORGOTTEN MAN

If you were asked who the third Vice President of the United States was, few would know it was Aaron Burr.

Wait a minute, didn't he shoot Alexander Hamilton in a duel?

Hamilton prominently takes his place in history as founder of what today is the Federal Reserve, the U.S. Mint, and with his picture on the $10 bill. Conversely, Burr's bio is found in very few school history books, primarily because of his 1807 duel.

Burr served during the Revolutionary War under Gen. Benedict Arnold in the Quebec expedition. Burr distinguished himself in the battle earning a place on Gen. George Washington's staff. But, after only two weeks, he asked for a transfer back to the battlefield.

In battle, Burr saved an entire brigade, which included Alexander Hamilton, from capture after the British landed on Manhattan. Evidently miffed because Burr had resigned from his staff, Washington did not commend Burr for his heroic actions. This led to an eventually estrangement between the two men.

In 1777, Burr was promoted to lieutenant colonel, assuming command of a regiment. During the harsh winter at Valley Forge,

Burr led a small unit guarding an isolated pass. He drove back an attempted mutiny by troops who wanted to escape the Valley Forge winter.

In 1779, Burr had to leave the Army due to bad health, but he remained active in the War. He was assigned by Washington to perform occasional intelligence missions. During one of those missions, Burr rallied a group of Yale students in New Haven, Conn., to aid a small group of soldiers in a skirmish with the British. This action repelled the enemy's advance, forcing them to retreat.

He was admitted to the bar of New York in 1782. He was twice elected to the New York state Assembly, was appointed State Attorney General, then he was chosen as a U.S. senator.

In those days, the office of President was elected by the Senate. Burr ran for President against Jefferson, but lost by one vote, relegating him to the office of Vice President, which second-place finishers became. Burr blamed Hamilton for his defeat.

In business, Burr founded the Bank of Manhattan Company, which today is JP Morgan-Chase. Hamilton founded rival Bank of New York, making them bitter political and business competitors.

It's the duel that caused Burr to be banished to obscurity. What caused the duel is a matter of conjecture. One of the reasons could be Hamilton's vicious rumors.

The two men were often invited to dinner parties hosted by leading New York politicians, businessmen, and even each other. During those years, Burr was widowed and lived with his daughter and her husband. Hamilton reportedly suggested Burr committed incest with his daughter. Enraged, the Vice President challenged the Treasury Secretary to a duel in Weehawken, New Jersey. Hamilton was mortally wounded, dying a day later. Hamilton's death destroyed Burr's political career.

Years later, Burr traveled west to embark upon what was an alleged attempt to form a new country, for which he was charged with treason, but was acquitted.

Burr spent the remainder of his life in obscurity practicing law in New York, dying in 1836.

7 AMERICA'S FIRST SPY NETWORK

Abraham Woodhull, a Long Island farmer from Setauket, was the leading civilian member of the so-called "American Culper Spy Ring," created by George Washington during the American Revolution.

The ring was headed up by Continental Army Major Benjamin Tallmadge. Woodhull, one of the ring's first recruits, used the alias "Samuel Culper," taken from Culpeper County, Virginia, Washington's home colony.

From 1778, through the end of the War, the British were headquartered in and operating out of New York City. Because of heavy taxes levied by the British, a great deal of smuggling by privateers (pirates) was conducted by the colonists. Woodhull was arrested for smuggling across Long Island Sound to Connecticut, which gave Major Tallmadge the opportunity to recruit his neighbor as a civilian spy.

Tallmadge persuaded Connecticut Governor, Jonathan Trumbull to release Woodhull, who soon agreed to join the spy ring. To protect his cover, Woodhull swore allegiance to the British crown and began making trips to Manhattan, gathering intelligence and sending his "Samuel Culper" letters to Washington.

Major Tallmadge developed a code to communicate with members of the ring that most member of the British forces would be unable to decode. This code was a series of letters and numbers that could make an ordinary message look like gibberish. In some of his letters, Woodhull used a type of invisible ink invented by Sir James Jay, brother of John Jay. To be read, the letter containing the ink needed to be brushed with iron sulfate, rather than just passed over heat or light. These measures helped maintain secrecy and ease Woodhull's anxiety about possibly being detected.

In New York, Woodhull would collect information from various sources, including British officers staying at a boarding house where he would lodge in New York. Then he would return to Setauket and pass the information to whaleboat operator Caleb Brewster, who would take the message across Long Island Sound to Major Tallmadge, who would then send the information to Washington.

The initial plan had problems. Woodhull's trips supposedly were to visit his sister, but the visits became too frequent, especially given the danger at the time. To further suspicions by the British, Woodhull, instead of being with his sister, he spent all of the time wandering the city without an obvious purpose, suggesting there was another reason he traveled to New York. The British became very suspicious by the spring of 1779.

Woodhull came up with a new plan and recruited Robert Townsend, who lived at his sister's boardinghouse. Woodhull discovered Townsend was a secret patriot, having been radicalized by British atrocities in his hometown of Oyster Bay. On June 20, 1779, Townsend sent his first report under the name of "Samuel Culper, Junior." As a resident, Townsend was better suited to spy in Manhattan. Moreover, his mercantile background gave him a good reason to inquire about British troop movements and shipping.

The American Culper Spy Ring was instrumental in uncovering General Benedict Arnold as a traitor by going over to the British.

This is a long, complex story throughout the Revolutionary War years and too long to put down in the space allotted. In AMC's current Revolutionary War TV spy-drama series, *"Turn: Washington's Spies,"* is based on Alexander Rose's historical book *"Washington's Spies: The Story of America's First Spy Ring"* (2007).

8 'THE FOX' HAD THE BRITISH ON THE RUN

During the Revolutionary War, the British were perplexed and confused by a new style of combat: guerrilla warfare. At the heart of what the British called "ungentlemanly" combat was South Carolinian farmer-turned-military officer, Francis Marion.

Serving with the Continental Army as a South Carolina militia officer, he was a persistent adversary of the British in South Carolina. He is considered the father of modern guerrilla warfare, and is credited in the lineage of the United States Army Rangers. He is known in history as the "Swamp Fox."

In 1775, Marion was commissioned a captain in the 2nd South Carolina Regiment under the command of William Moultrie. He rose to the rank of lieutenant colonel. Marion became known for his leadership abilities and was sent to join the command of Major General Horatio Gates just before the Battle of Camden. Gates was less than impressed and promptly sent Marion to take command of the Williamsburg militia in Virginia.

Thinking Marion would be kept out of the way, Gates assigned him to scouting missions. Marion showed himself to be an able leader of irregular militiamen and ruthless tactics in terrorizing of

British loyalists.

Unlike George Washington's Continental troops, "Marion's Men," as they were known, served without pay, supplied their own horses, arms and often their food.

Marion rarely committed his men to a frontal attack style of warfare, but repeatedly surprised larger bodies of Loyalists or British regulars with quick surprise attacks and equally quick withdrawal from the field. In other words, his tactics were ambush-style "hit and run," befuddling the British.

The British especially hated Marion and made repeated efforts to neutralize his force, but Marion's intelligence-gathering was excellent, whereas that of the British was poor, due to the overwhelming patriot loyalty of the populace in the Williamsburg area.

In November 1780, the British had their own "head-hunter" in Colonel Banastre Tarleton, who was sent to capture or kill Marion. Tarleton found it no easy task in finding the "old swamp fox." Marion eluded him by traveling along swamp paths. It was Tarleton who gave Marion the moniker when, after unsuccessfully pursuing Marion's troops for over 26 miles through a swamp. Tarleton gave up and swore "... as for this damned old fox, the Devil himself could not catch him."

Once Marion had shown his ability at guerrilla warfare, making himself a serious nuisance to the British, South Carolina Govenor John Rutledge commissioned him a brigadier general of his state's militia.

In January 1782, he left the fighting when he was elected to a new South Carolina State Assembly. Later that year, the British withdrew their garrison from Charleston and the war was brought to an end by the Treaty of Paris.

Marion is one of those characters in history who is surrounded by controversy. Many of his exploits have been exaggerated. His legend was helped along by a popular 1959 Walt Disney TV series, "The Swamp Fox," starring Leslie Nielsen. In 2000, actor Mel

Gibson starred in "The Patriot," whose character was based on Marion's legend.

But when studying the legend of "The Swamp Fox," consider the words of legendary film director, John Ford: "If given the choice between filming truth or legend, choose the legend, it's always more interesting."

9 THE WHOLE SHEBANG, LOCK, STOCK & BARREL

The American and English languages (yes, there is a distinct difference), we have used curious sayings that emanated from activities and social experiences.

Example where someone might say regarding a person receiving a number of items:

*"You've got the entire amount… take the whole **Kit and Caboodle** … lock, stock and barrel."*

Back in the pre-Revolutionary War days, if you wanted to buy a musket (rifle), you had to go to three separate vendors – a barrel maker (blacksmith), a carpenter who carved the gun stock, and a maker of "flint locks" (the mechanism that includes the firing hammer and the lock that ignites the gun power to fire the weapon). Self-assembly was required.

As for **Kit and Caboodle**, that source is unknown.

To play *"**Cat and Mouse**"* with someone comes from early 20th century England when Parliament passed a law called the "Prisoners Discharge For Ill-Health Act." It promptly became known as the *"Cat & Mouse Act."* Hunger strikers would be released from prison because of ill-health, but could be re-arrested when they recovered.

Indian Giver: With the history of our nation regarding our ill-treatment of Native Americans, this term is self-explanatory.

The term *"Break the Ice,"* goes back more than four centuries when, at the beginning of spring, river boaters would break the ice in order to make passage. The more modern usage comes from the 1823 poems of "Don Juan" by Lord Byron, referring to the British people: *"… and your cold people are beyond all price, once you've broken their confounded ice."*

In seafaring folklore, *"Davy Jones' Locker,"* refers to a sailor's hell beneath the sea. The verbiage comes from a book, "The Adventures of Peregrine Pickle," written in 1751, by Tobias Smollett. In Chapter XIII, Peregrine and two fellow sailors attempt to frighten Commodore Trinnion by a dreaded ghost, which the trio had concocted. It worked so well that Trinnion was frightened one evening by exclaiming: *"I'll be damned if it wasn't Davy Jones himself! I know him by his huge saucer eyes, his three rows of teeth and tail and the blue smoke that came out of his nostrils."* According to seafaring mythology, Davy Jones sits on the rigging during hurricanes and storms warning of death and disaster.

To call someone *"Mad as a Hatter,"* refers to a person not in their right mind, but did that term come from Lewis Carroll's 1865 book *"Alice in Wonderland?"* No. it was used long before Carroll's book. Hat makers used mercury in manufacturing head-wear. After years of toiling in a hat factory, workers would often become mentally ill from mercury poisoning. The term was used to describe one of Carroll's main characters.

It's so cold it could *"Freeze the Balls Off a Brass Monkey"* is a sailing warship term, contrary to those in modern times who try to make it an indecent remark. Sailing warships of the 16th through 19th centuries were armed with cannons. Alongside each cannon were brass platforms, known as "monkeys," holding stacks of cannon balls, making them conveniently available for gunners mates to grab them quickly to reload. With this explanation, during cold weather, the saying is self-explanatory.

"To Burn One's Bridges" comes from the days of Caesar. When he would invade a country to conquer it, Caesar would burn all bridges his armies used to cross into the foreign territory. To Caesar, retreat was not an option. The burning of bridges was an incentive used for his officers and soldiers, giving them no alternative but to push ahead and conquer the enemy.

10 THE FOUNDING OF MISSION SAN LUIS REY

The Spanish military and priests determined a new Spanish mission was needed to cut the travel time between San Diego and San Juan Capistrano.

Father Fermin de Lausen founded Mission San Luis Rey on June 13, 1798.

The Spanish tried to position the 21 missions along, or close to, the coast so each could easily be reached within a day's travel on horseback, mule, and foot along California original highway, El Camino Real (the royal road). The travel distance between each mission was approximately 30 miles.

El Camino Real began as little more than a footpath, but nonetheless a coastal passage for travel from San Diego to San Francisco. Portions of the original route exist today from San Diego north to San Francisco in a variety of highway and various city street fashion.

There is good documentation of a visit by British explorer George Vancouver. He described San Diego as a less-than-desirable place to live. He found the Spanish to be rather cool in their hospitality, and the balmy coastal climate not to his liking. "The way of life in California," according to Vancouver's journal, "is not calculated to produce any great increase in white inhabitants."

Mission San Luis Rey de Francia was laid out and built some five miles east of the coast line along the south shore of the San Luis Rey River. It was named in honor of King Louis 9th of France, who had been a Franciscan friar.

No figure in California mission history is more revered by the Luiseno people than is Father Antonio Peyri. By late summer of 1798, some 6,000 adobe bricks had been made for the new church, which was completed by 1802.

At the height of mission San Luis Rey's dominance in north county, it was the largest of the 21 complexes and the most prosperous, with some 25,000 head of cattle, 26,000 sheep, 2,000 head of horses, all maintained by 5,000 Luiseños living in and around the mission. At one time it was the largest civilized living and working complex west of the Mississippi. Mission San Luis Rey became known as "King of the Missions."

The Mexicans take control...

In 1821, the Mexican people overthrew some 300 years of Spanish rule.

The new Mexican government insisted upon separating church and state, which meant the demise of the mission system and its vast holdings. Secularization meant the holdings of land and livestock at each mission was taken by the new government and sold to the public.

More importantly, the Padres at each of the missions no longer had control over the native population. The mostly Spanish-born Padres refused to swear allegiance to the new Republic of Mexico, which caused them to be feared and distrusted by Mexican officials.

Mexican secularization made all mission property public, and the natives were to be freed. This move, however, made the wealth that had been built up by each mission open to politicians and their cronies to grab the riches for little or nothing, all under the semblance of law. It could be compared with the "reconstruction" period in the South after the American Civil War.

During the secularization period in Mexico and Alta California there was a rapid increase in the number of private ranchos. Here in North County, Rancho Los Flores y Santa Margarita today is known as Camp Pendleton. Rancho Guajome in Vista was a subsidiary of Margarita.

Mission San Luis Rey was abandoned and surrendered to the Mexican government in 1835, clearing the way for officers, soldiers, and landowners to loot or buy off at ridiculously cheap prices the vast holdings of the mission.

The looting became so fierce that even the huge timber beams holding up the roof of the church and other major buildings were stolen by ranchers to construct their own private buildings. For the next century, artifacts taken by the Mexicans during the period were gradually found in private homes and collections, much of which has been returned to the Mission.

Mexico's neglected Alta California might never have become part of the United States had it not been for three visionaries with very huge egos: Colonel John C. Fremont, Commodore Robert F. Stockton, and Brigadier General Stephen W. Kearny.

Because it could take as long as six months to get a message to and from Washington, D.C., decisions had to be made on the spot, at the moment of opportunity. The question of who really had control of California wasn't settled for some time. The population's attitude was mixed. A good deal of the people welcomed U.S. control; the landowners with huge Spanish and Mexican land grants were less than eager to see a governmental change. Today, Mission San Luis Rey sits in the center of Oceanside and continues to be an active place of worship, education, and retreat.

11 THE RISE AND FALL OF NAPOLEON BONAPARTE

After King Louis XVI and his wife, Marie Antoinette, were executed, chaos reigned over France. Neighboring nations such as Austria, Prussia (Germany), Spain, and Great Britain declared war on France.

After the Revolution's "Reign of Terror" during which much of France's aristocracy and leaders had been executed or imprisoned, a young artillery officer quickly rose through the ranks capturing the hearts of his countrymen much as he had overwhelmed his enemies on the field of battle. Napoleon was quick to capitalize on his popularity. He became known as "The Little Corporal," which referred to where he started in the Grand Army and his short stature.

Firmly in control of the army, which meant he controlled the nation, in 1804, Napoleon was crowned Emperor of France. During the coronation ceremony in Paris' historic Notre Dame cathedral, the Little Corporal did something that shocked everyone witnessing the ceremony: just as the pope was about to place the crown on his head, Napoleon grabbed it, and put it on himself. He would later explain that no mortal man was above the Emperor, so how could anyone but Napoleon himself place the crown?

With Napoleon firmly in control of what would soon become the most powerful army in Europe, France went on the offensive, conquering nearly all of Europe and much of Russia. Because of early explorers and fur trappers, France controlled half of what is today the continental United States, plus much of the middle portion of settled Canada. The only thing stopping him from complete European domination was the British Royal Navy, the most powerful in the world. In order to raise money to build up his army and navy, Napoleon sold all of France's territory to the United States in 1803. The prairie land between the Mississippi River, from New Orleans, which was France's Louisiana capital city, north and west to the Rockies and Canada were included. It became known as "The Louisiana Purchase." The selling price was a staggering $15 million, less than 3 cents an acre. Today, nearly all of this land produces enough food to feed millions of people around the world.

In 1805, Napoleon lost a critical sea battle at Cape Trafalgar off the coast of Spain. Realizing his Grand Army could never cross the English Channel as long as the Royal Navy controlled the seas, Napoleon marched his Grand Army across Europe, invading Russia. Just as Hitler would do a century and a half later, Napoleon over reached his capabilities. He out-ran his supply lines, and being ill-equipped for winter, the weather and Russia's "scorched earth" tactic (burning everything and then retreating, leaving nothing for the enemy to survive on), Napoleon had to retreat from Moscow in 1812.

Napoleon was harassed and attacked by Cossacks all during the retreat to the Russian border. He entered Russia with 600,000 troops, but only 40,000 survived to return home. Napoleon returned to France where he was stripped of his crown and exiled to Elba, a small, desolate Mediterranean island off the coast of Italy. Napoleon was given a personal guard of 600 French troops, but the sea around Elba was patrolled by the Royal Navy. He managed to escape and return to power.

In 1815, Napoleon led his reorganized Grand Army against the British and the Duke of Wellington at the Battle of Waterloo in present-day Belgium. Once again in defeat, he was stripped of his power and exiled to the even smaller and more desolate British-owned island of St. Helena in the South Atlantic off the coast of Africa where he died mysteriously on or before May 15, 1821. It's long been a debate whether he died of natural causes or was murdered. This is one of history's great mysteries.

ONE MORE THING...

Napoleon's influence is still around us today. Every nation Napoleon conquered or controlled drives its vehicles on the right side of the road. The British drive on the left side of road. The reason has been argued, but the most common explanation is that Napoleon wanted his cavalry to be able draw their swords and fight as they road down a road with the weapon on the "outside of the column, instead of the inside. It makes sense if everyone was right-handed. Still, like his death, no one knows for sure. And, why you ask, do we, as well as Canada, Mexico, and Latin America drive on the right? Remember, France at one time controlled half of Canada before the British took it away from them. Mexico and all of South America were conquered by Spain and Portugal, both of whom were allies of France.

As far as the United States is concerned, I figure it was just contrariness on the part of our Founding Fathers not to stay on the left, but take the right course. Ask any Brit about driving on the left and they'll explain, "You Americans drive on the right side of the road, whereas we British drive on the 'correct' side of the road.

IT'S OUR MANIFEST DESTINY

12 THE BUYING OF OUR HEARTLAND

The 1803 acquisition by the U.S. of 828,000 square miles or nearly 530 million acres in the center of the North American continent was French territory known as "Louisiana."

The U.S. paid $11.250 million in cash plus cancellation of French debts amounting to $3.75 million for a total sum of $15 million, amounting to around 3 to 4 cents per acre. In today's money that's about $236 million, or less than 42 cents per acre.

The Louisiana territory encompassed all or part of 15 present U.S. states and two Canadian provinces. The land purchased contained all of present-day Arkansas, Missouri, Iowa, Oklahoma, Kansas, and Nebraska; parts of Minnesota that were west of the Mississippi River; most of North Dakota; most of South Dakota; northeastern New Mexico; northern Texas; the portions of Montana, Wyoming, and Colorado east of the Continental Divide; Louisiana west of the Mississippi River, including the city of New Orleans; and small portions of land that would eventually become part of the Canadian provinces of Alberta and Saskatchewan.

Under Napoleon Bonaparte, France planned on building an empire in North America. A slave revolt in Haiti, and an impending war with Britain, however, led Napoleon to abandon those plans and sell the entire territory to the United States. Interestingly enough, the U.S. entered negotiations intending just to buy New Orleans and it's the surrounding lands.

Jefferson had concerns that a U.S. President did not have the constitutional authority to make such a deal. He also thought that to do so would erode states' rights by increasing federal executive power. On the other hand, he was aware of the potential French threat and was prepared to go to war to prevent a strong French presence there.

In 1802, James Monroe and Robert R. Livingston traveled to Paris to negotiate with Napoleon for the purchase of New Orleans. History now shows the Louisiana Purchase is considered one of Thomas Jefferson's greatest contributions to the nation.

In 1801, Napoleon had sent a military force to secure New Orleans, putting fear in plantation owners that he would free the slaves.

Jefferson was wary of what the French emperor might do next, so he gave Livingston and Monroe instructions to go to London to negotiate an alliance if the Louisiana talks in Paris failed.

On April 11, 1803, Napoleon abruptly offered Livingston and Monroe all of Louisiana Territory for $15 million. The American representatives were dumbfounded with the offer. They were prepared to pay up to $10 million for only New Orleans, but when the vastly larger territory was offered for $15 million, Livingston and Monroe realized the bargain – a chance to double the size of the country at a very small cost. They were certain Jefferson and the Congress would accept the offer.

The American diplomats feared Napoleon might withdraw the offer at any time, preventing the United States from obtaining their primary goal: New Orleans. So, on April 30, 1803, the agreement was signed, doubling the size of the nation and the Louisiana Territory became U.S. property. It contained far more than just New Orleans, which was the goal.

Ironically, on July 4, 1803, the nation's 27th birthday, the treaty reached Washington, D.C. Later that year, Jefferson sent Merriweather Lewis and William Clark on an exploratory trek across the newly-acquired real estate to the Pacific Ocean, detailing what the nation owned.

13 JOHN C. FREMONT:
PATHFINDER TO THE WEST

More than any other American, John Charles Fremont accomplished far-reaching feats, which not only resulted in the settling of the American West, but were instrumental in the founding of California.

There isn't enough space to detail Fremont's many accomplishments, as well as blunders and controversial decisions attributed to him. He held a controversial appointment as the first U.S. governor of California, and later was elected as one of the state's first two U.S. senators. He was appointed to explore the West by Presidential order, convicted of mutiny in an Army court martial, only to become the first presidential candidate of the Republican Party.

Along with Washington, Jefferson, and Lincoln, the name "Fremont" can be found throughout the nation titling cities, counties, streets, schools, libraries, and even a football championship trophy between universities in Nevada.

Historians portray Frémont as controversial, impetuous, and contradictory. Some scholars regard him as a military hero of significant accomplishment, while others view him as a failure.

Nevertheless, Fremont became popularly known as America's "Pathfinder."

In 1841, Frémont married Jessie Benton, daughter of Missouri's U.S. Sen. Thomas Hart Benton, who was the Democratic Party's leader for more than 30 years in the Senate. Benton championed the Western expansionist movement known as "Manifest Destiny," which was a belief the North American continent should belong to the United States.

The public embraced "The Pathfinder's" vision of the West as a place of wide open and inviting lands to be settled. The Mormans were lured to Utah because of Fremont's reports.

In 1846, war broke out with Mexico. Acting on orders from U.S. Navy Commodore Robert F. Stockton, Major Fremont led an expedition of 300 men to capture Santa Barbara and Los Angeles. Fremont accepted the surrender of California by Mexican Gov. Andres Pico, putting it under U.S. control. Stockton then appointed Fremont military governor.

But trouble developed out of that appointment. Fremont was challenged by an old foe, Brig. Gen. Stephen Watts Kearny, who claimed he had been appointed governor by President Polk. Fremont refused to step aside, but Kearny pulled rank and ordered the major to report back to Washington, D.C., to stand court-martial. He was convicted of mutiny, disobedience of a superior officer and military misconduct.

Because of Fremont's many accomplishments, Polk quickly commuted the sentence to a dishonorable discharge.

Fremont returned to California and got rich in the gold fields. Then, in 1850, upon the admission of California into the Union, Frémont was elected to serve as one of the state's first two senators.

In 1856, the GOP nominated Fremont as their first presidential candidate. He lost the election to Democrat James Buchanan, but when the Civil War broke out, President Lincoln appointed Fremont a brigadier general in command of the Army of the West based in St. Louis.

While there, Frémont saw great potential in a relatively unknown militia general, U.S. Grant. Fremont put Grant in command of an expedition to secure the Mississippi River. From that success, Grant went on to be the Union's top and most successful general – thanks for Fremont's foresight.

Years later, President Rutherford Hayes appointed Fremont Governor of the Arizona Territory where he served for four years.

On July 13, 1890, Frémont, 77, died in New York.

John C. Fremont's story was written in detail by author David Nevin (not the actor) in his book "Dream West," which later was made into a TV mini-series starring Richard Chamberlain.

14 LAFITTE: THE SCOUNDREL OR HERO?

French-American Jean Lafitte was a pirate who has been referred to as both a scoundrel and hero. Jean and his brother, Pierre Lafitte, had a fleet of ships, as well as operating a New Orleans smuggling and warehouse operation in the early 1800s.

Born in 1780, Jean Lafitte and Pierre used their warehouse to disperse their smuggled goods, but after the United States government passed the Embargo Act of 1807, the Lafittes moved their operations to an island in Barataria Bay south of New Orleans.

Jean Lafitte's name became famous for his role during the War of 1812. While history does not argue with the pirate's participation on the high seas, there has been controversy as to how much of a contribution Lafitte made to help General Andrew Jackson defeat the British during the Battle of New Orleans. Ironically, because of the length of time required for news from Europe to reach America, the the war had been over three months when the battle occurred.

As the story goes, Jackson met with Lafitte, who offered to serve if the U.S. would pardon those of his men who would fight to defend the city. Jackson agreed. With Lafitte's encouragement, many of his men joined the New Orleans militia or as sailors to man the ships. Others formed three artillery companies.

On Dec. 23, 1814, advance units of the British fleet reached the Mississippi River. Lafitte realized that the American line of defense was so short as potentially to allow the British to encircle the American troops. Lafitte suggested the line of defense be extended to a nearby swamp, and Jackson ordered it done.

On land and sea, the pirate gunners earned praise as the battle continued. Jackson praised Jean and Pierre Lafitte for having

"… exhibited courage and fidelity." The future president formally requested clemency for the Lafittes and the men who had served under them. The U.S. government granted Jackson's request with a full pardon for all on Feb. 6, 1815.

Given the pirate's legendary reputation, there was much wild speculation about whether, or how, Lafitte died. Rumors abounded: some say he changed his name and disappeared; others that he was killed by his own men shortly after leaving Galveston, Texas; or, a ridiculous story that he rescued French Emperor Napoleon and they both died in Louisiana. While there were no authentic records of Jean Lafitte's death, it is generally believed he died sometime in 1823.

Today, festivals, streets, and parks are named for the pirate. Lafitte's Blacksmith Shop bar is located on Bourbon Street in New Orleans. Constructed prior to 1732, the structure is believed to be the oldest bar in the United States.

Jean Lafitte remains an enigmatic character of American history. Whether he was a hero or scoundrel is left for historical interpretation. There's little doubt that he has captured the imagination of writers, both historian and novelists, as well as Hollywood, with three films depicting his "supposed exploits."

15 DOLLEY MADISON:
FIRST HOSTESS OF THE UNITED STATES

When we think of grand First Ladies of the White House, Jackie Kennedy is probably the first image that comes to mind. Nancy Reagan leads a short list of other First Ladies, but when the White House was finally completed in the very early 19th century, it was President James Madison's wife, Dolley, who set the standard most chief executives' wives have followed since.

Dolley and James Madison occupied the White from 1809 to 1817. She was noted for her social gifts, which boosted her husband's popularity. She did much to define the role of the President's wife, but ironically, it wasn't only for her husband, but for the widowed President Thomas Jefferson before the Madisons moved in.

Born Dolley Payne on May 20, 1768, in New Garden, North Carolina, it was after the War of 1812, she re-furnished the reconstructed White House. The executive mansion was first occupied by President John and Abigail Adams, but the interior was unfinished and unfurnished until Jefferson moved in. Work continued on the White House through the Jefferson administration.

Dolley Payne Todd and James Madison, a congressman from Virginia, probably met at social events in Philadelphia. Reportedly, Aaron Burr, a longtime friend of Madison's since their student days at Princeton University, stayed at a rooming house where Dolley, a widow, lived. In May 1794, Burr made the formal introduction between the young widow and Madison, who was 17 years her senior. After a brief courtship, they were married on Sept. 15, 1794.

It was during the War of 1812, Dolley became a heroine. In 1814, as the enemy approached the city, Dolley is credited with saving the classic portrait of George Washington, along with a number of other national household treasures. However, in recent years that claim has been challenged. Popular accounts during and after the war years tended to portray Dolley Madison as the one who removed the painting. Early 20th century historians note that Jean Pierre Sioussat, a Frenchman, had directed the servants to remove the painting.

In 1815, after the war, Congress allowed "Madame Dolley Madison a refurbishing allowance of $14,000 to purchase new furniture for the Executive Mansion."

While James Madison is the leading architect of the U.S. Constitution, like Jefferson, their legacies are tainted because they were slave holders.

After James' death on June 28 1836, Dolley remained at their Montpelier plantation for a year. During that time, she organized and copied her husband's papers. Congress authorized $55,000 as payment for seven volumes, including his notes on the Constitutional Convention.

In the fall of 1837, Dolley Madison returned to Washington. She moved into a house, on Lafayette Square. Dolley took her slave butler Paul Jennings with her, forcing him to leave his family in Virginia.

While living in Washington, Dolley tried to raise money by

selling the rest of Madison's papers. She also agreed to sell Jennings to Daniel Webster, who allowed Jennings to gain his freedom by paying Webster through work.

Unable to find a buyer for the remaining Madison papers, she sold Montpelier, the remaining slaves, and the furnishings to pay off outstanding debts.

In the last days of her life, Dolley was in absolute poverty. Webster often sent Jennings to visit Dolley with food and telling the slave whenever he saw anything she needed to take it to her. In some cases, Jennings would give her money out of his own pocket. In 1848, Congress agreed to buy the rest of James Madison's papers for around $25,000.

On July 12, 1849, Dolley Madison died at age 81, in her Washington D.C., home. She was first buried in the Congressional Cemetery, Washington, but later moved to a grave at Montpelier plantation next to her husband.

16 THE BLACK HAWK WAR

When it comes to the American Indian wars, little has been said, written, or filmed about those conflicts that occurred in America's Middle West. In 1832, one particular conflict saw a 23-year-old Abraham Lincoln serving for a short time as an elected militia captain in what would become known as "The Black Hawk War."

Black Hawk was a Sauk War Chief who rallied remnants of three tribes to take back lands in Illinois they claimed had been unfairly taken.

In addition to Lincoln, other notable participants in The Black Hawk War included Army officers Winfield Scott, Zachary Taylor, and Jefferson Davis. Davis, was the son-in-law of future President Zachary Taylor. Davis would become the leader of the rebelling Confederate States during the Civil War.

The Black Hawk War gave impetus to the U.S. policy of Indian removal, in which Native American tribes were pressured to sell their lands and move west of the Mississippi River.

The war erupted soon after Black Hawk, who was in his sixties, led a combined group of some 6,000 Sauks, Meskwakis (Fox), and Kickapoos known as the "British Band." In April 1832, they crossed the Mississippi River back into the Illinois from Iowa.

The "British Band" moniker was for those tribes fighting with the British against the U.S. in the War of 1812.

Black Hawk was hoping to avoid bloodshed while resettling on tribal land that had been supposedly given to the United States in the disputed 1804 "Treaty of St. Louis." The tribes believed they had been duped. The St. Louis agreement had been negotiated by future President William Henry Harrison, who then was governor of the Missouri territory at the time. A group of Sauk and Meskwakis (Fox) leaders supposedly "sold" their lands east of the Mississippi in Illinois for more than $2,200, in goods and annual payments of $1,000 in supplies.

The treaty became controversial because the tribal leaders had not been authorized by their councils to give up lands. The chiefs probably did not intend to give up "ownership" or they would not have sold so much territory for such a small price. The treaty's included more territory than the Indians realized, but tribal leaders didn't learn the true extent of the treaty until the early 1830s.

When the river crossing took place, U.S. officials were convinced Black Hawk and his followers were hostile. Accordingly, on May 14, 1832, an Illinois militia opened fire on an Indian delegation. Black Hawk responded by successfully attacking the militia at the Battle of Stillman's Run. He then led his band to a secure location in what is now southern Wisconsin. From there he was pursued by the militia and a contingent of U.S. troops..

The militia, led by Col. Henry Dodge, caught up with Black Hawk on July 21 and defeated him at the Battle of Wisconsin Heights, forcing the Indians to retreat.

Black Hawk's band had been weakened by hunger, death, and desertion. Many of the survivors retreated to the Mississippi River. On Aug. 2, 1832, U.S. soldiers attacked the remnants of Black Hawk's followers at the Battle of Bad Axe, killing many or capturing most of those who survived, but Black Hawk and other tribal leaders escaped. They later surrendered and were imprisoned for a year.

Shortly before being released from custody, Black Hawk told his life story to an interpreter, and in 1833, was published -- the first Native American autobiography to be published. It became an immediate bestseller and went through several editions. Black Hawk died in 1838 (at age 70 or 71) in what is now southeastern Iowa.

With the Black Hawk War concluded, President Andrew Jackson forced most of those Native Americans resisting the white man's way-of-life to give up all their lands east of the Mississippi River. The Indian wars with the Great Plains tribes and those of the Southwest would continue throughout much of the rest of the 19th century.

For those Native Americans east of the Mississippi, Black Hawk joins Tecumseh as being two of the great leaders who stood up to the white man's invasion.

17 THE IOWA-MISSOURI HONEY WAR

When Robert Lucas assumed the duties as Iowa's territorial governor in the 1830s, he found a serious border dispute brewing. The issue: the boundary between Iowa and Missouri. Iowa's first governor had been in office less than two years when the two states' militias were faced off, ready to go to war.

When Missouri became a State in 1820, her northern boundary was the latitude passing through the "rapids of the river Des Moines." At the time, the land along that boundary was in the possession of Native American tribes, but when they were removed some years later, Missouri took steps to establish exact limits.

In 1836, Missouri declared the "rapids in the Des Moines River and the parallel of latitude indicated that which ran through the great bend in the Des Moines River near Keosauqua, Iowa."

For many years the term "Des Moines Rapids" had been taken to mean the rapids in the Mississippi, just above the mouth of the Des Moines. Travelers, settlers, river men, and even the Indians, called them the "Des Moines Rapids." To add more confusion, the southern boundary of Iowa was defined by the U.S. Congress as "the northern boundary of Missouri."

Missouri claimed a strip of land some 13 miles wide, which today forms Iowa's southern border. The people living in Southern Iowa and Northern Missouri were of hearty pioneer stock and paid little attention to law, but when a Missouri sheriff tried to collect taxes on honey trees in what he considered being in his Clarke County, Iowa settlers claimed he was out of his jurisdiction and arrested him.

When the attempt to levy taxes was rebuffed, the Missouri governor ordered 1,000 militia to uphold what he deemed "the dignity of the State."

Governor Lucas, of Iowa Territory, himself a soldier, had successfully settled a similar contest when he was governor of Ohio. Ohio and Michigan, quarreled over a piece of land known as the "Toledo Strip." He was quick to react in this matter. Lucas called for the Iowa militia to repel an invasion by Missouri.

The settlements in Iowa Territory of 1839, were scattered with a poorly organized militia. But within a short time, the call to arms brought 500 Hawkeyes bearing down on the Missourians. The two forces were glaring at each other, anxious for a fight.

Fortunately no one was hurt. The Iowans sent a peace commission into Missouri. The result: Clarke County's levying of taxes was withdrawn. A committee was dispatched to present the Iowa Territorial Legislature in Burlington with a proposal for friendly arbitration. Hawkeye troops were withdrawn and the Iowa Legislature agreed to a peace treaty.

But, although war was averted, the dispute wasn't settled. It wasn't until Jan. 3, 1851, did the U.S. Supreme Court make a final ruling. Iowa won. The Supreme Court did not accept the claims of either side as to the rapids. It was an old Indian boundary line run by a government surveyor in 1816, that was selected as the proper one. The eastern terminus of the boundary came farther south below the point insisted by Missouri, which satisfied Iowa.

The question was decided just in time because Missouri was a slave State and Iowa was "free" of slavery. A boundary such as the one between the two states was vital.

Because the land claimed by both Iowa and Missouri was, for the most part, heavily wooded and rich in bee trees. The quarrel became known as the "Honey War." Many jokes were made between Iowans and Missourians about the contest; frontier poets wrote about it, and stories were circulated for years about the time when Iowa and Missouri nearly went to war over a little bit 'o honey.

18 'OLD HICTORY' – A NOT SO NICE MAN

When you think of Andrew Jackson, and probably not many of you do, three things come to mind: He defeated the British in the Battle of New Orleans; he was the 7th President of the United States; and his portrait graces the 20 dollar bill.

A veteran of the Revolutionary War, Jackson was a tough-as-nails frontiersman who was a lawyer and one of the founders of the state of Tennessee. He was elected to represent Tennessee in the U.S. House of Representatives, and later to the U.S. Senate.

After the 1814 defeat of the British, he and his militia were transferred to Florida to run out the Spanish, who had held the peninsula for more than two centuries.

NOTE: The War of 1812 had been over by three months when Jackson's forces defeated the British at New Orleans. It took that long for word to reach Jackson from the peace table in Ghet, Belgium.

Jackson was nominated for president in 1824, but narrowly was defeated by John Quincy Adams. Four years later, Jackson ran again as a nominee of the newly-founded Democrat Party and decisively defeated Adams, but not without a cost. The campaign became so dirty that Jackson's wife, Rachel, died of a stroke due to attacks against her. She never got to serve as First Lady.

There had always been a cloud over the Jackson marriage with an accusation that Rachel had committed bigamy. Thinking her first marriage had been terminated by divorce, she married Jackson. But her first husband, Lewis Robards, had never completed the divorce. When the Jacksons found out, Rachel got the divorce and remarried Jackson.

Jackson had a contentious rivalry with Senator Henry Clay, leader of the opposition Whig Party. The two hated each other; each never missed a chance to toss an insult. Clay served in both houses of Congress from neighboring Kentucky. He ran unsuccessfully three times (1824, 1832, and 1844). Clay dominated the Whig Party, which he founded. He served as Secretary of State in the John Quincy Adams' administration. Jackson's presence in Washington was overwhelming, but was overshadowed only by his nemesis, Henry Clay.

As President, Jackson curtailed an effort by South Carolina to secede from the Union, threatening military force if South Carolina leaders didn't back down. They did.

Jackson was an advocate of "Manifest Destiny," (the U.S. claim it had the right to expand across the continent), and he feared some of the Indian tribes would become extinct if care wasn't taken. Still, as President, Jackson enforced the Indian Removal Act, which relocated several tribes, including the Cherokee, from the Southeastern states of Georgia, South Carolina, and Alabama to the Indian Territory (now Oklahoma).

Though he faced, and defeated, Henry Clay in the 1832 Presidential Election, and opposed Clay generally, Jackson's presidency saw a substantial expansion in federal spending using Clay's "American System" program. Jackson's presidency also saw the development of the spoils system, the complete payoff of all federal debt, and the first assassination attempt on a president (which Jackson fought off himself).

His tough-as-nails demeanor and never-bend reputation

throughout his life earned Jackson the nickname of "Old' Hickory."

Jackson left office following the 1836 election of his vice president Martin Van Buren as President. Though his involvement in politics continued as he guided the Democratic Party against the Whigs, and even played a role in the 1844 election of James K. Polk as president, he spent the rest of his life in Tennessee and died in 1845.

19 THE GADSDEN PURCHASE

Looking at the map today of the Southwestern United States, approximately one-third of the lower part of Arizona and a portion of southern New Mexico was the last parcel added to the contiguous 48 states by what was known as the "Gadsden Purchase" from the Republic of Mexico.

In that $15 million Land transaction of 1853, the United States also came very close to possessing the entire peninsula of Baja California. But that would have cost the U.S. an additional $50 million for Baja if it was added to the territorial portions of the northern Mexican states of Sonora and Chihuahua. The Gadsden Purchase consisted of a 29,640 square-mile region of present-day southern Arizona and southwestern New Mexico.

The treaty was signed on Dec. 30, 1853 by James Gadsden, who at the time was the ambassador to Mexico. The treaty also served to reconcile outstanding border issues between the U.S. and Mexico emanating from the 1848 Treaty of Guadalupe Hidalgo, which ended the war with Mexico.

The treaty, known in Mexico as the "Sale of La Mesilla," was primarily negotiated to provide right-of-way for U.S. transcontinental railroads. The war had left Mexico heavily in debt. Yankee dollars were sorely needed by Mexican President Santa Anna, who wanted to rebuild his army out of fear the Americans would attack again.

The Gadsden Purchase was ratified, with changes, by the U.S. Senate on April 25, 1854, and signed by President Franklin Pierce, with final approval taken by Mexico's congress on June 8, 1854. The purchase included lands south of the Gila River and west of the Rio Grande, which make it possible for the U.S. to construct a transcontinental railroad with a southern route. Pre-Civil War business-oriented Southerners saw such a transcontinental railroad linking the southern U.S. states with the Pacific Coast, which would expand their trade opportunities.

However, many in Washington thought the topography of the southern portion of the original boundary line to the 1848 Mexican ceded territories, (California, Nevada, Utah, Arizona, New Mexico, western Colorado) were too mountainous to allow such a direct rail route.

President Pierce's administration, strongly influenced by Secretary of War Jefferson Davis, had seen an opportunity to acquire land for the railroad by adding a significant amount of territory from northern Mexico. However, controversial debate in Washington, D.C., developed over the treaty which evolved into a North-South dispute over slavery. Would the newly-acquired territory be allowed slavery?

After the treaty was approved by both countries, a survey party was designated to officially establish the border. The joint American-Mexican survey party surveyed and mapped the Gadsden Purchase border from the Pacific to El Paso. With that party was U.S. Army surveyor Lt. Cave Couts. He would later be one of the first white settlers to develop a vast Rancho Guajome located in what today is northern San Diego County. The surveyor's transit Couts used was, for a time, on display at the County's Rancho Guajome museum in Vista.

Today, the Gadsden Purchase and the Treaty of Guadalupe

Hidalgo have been nearly forgotten, but both are important aspects of American history. Our southern border would look very different today without the Gadsden Purchase, but how very different it would look if Baja California had been included in that treaty.

20 CAVE COUTS PIONEER OF SAN DIEGO'S NORTH COUNTY

He died at the Horton House, in San Diego, June 10 1874. He was over six feet tall, perfectly straight, and weighed 165 pounds. He was a man of good education, strict integrity, and gentlemanly manners. His widow continued to live on the rancho and manage it until her death. Their children were ten, of whom nine lived to maturity: Abel Stearns, who died in 1855, aged nearly four years; María Antonia, who was married to Chalmers Scott, and still lives in San Diego; William Bandini, who married Christina, daughter of Salvador Estudillo, and is a farmer living near San Marcos; Ysidora Forster, who was married to W.D. Gray; Elena, married to Parker Dear and lived several years on the Santa Rosa rancho; Robert Lee; John Forster; and Caroline.

In early spring of 1849, a twenty-seven-year-old army lieutenant, Cave Johnson Couts, arrived in southern California. As part of a detachment of American soldiers, he had been ordered to serve occupation duty following the recent war with Mexico.[1] At first detailed to Los Angeles, Couts later traveled to San Diego to assist joint Mexican and American efforts to survey a new boundary line between Upper and Lower California.[2] Unlike a fellow newcomer, who referred to the settlement as a "miserable Mexican town,"[3] Couts liked what he saw in San Diego and decided to remain. In 1851, he resigned his commission from the army and married Ysidora Bandini, the daughter of a prosperous local businessman. He established himself on a large rancho[4] and took up the life of a family man, ranchero, and civic leader.[5] In short, like many other Americans who came to California, Couts saw an opportunity for a fresh start and a chance to realize his ambitions.

Cave Couts is well known to San Diego historians as a result of his meticulous care in recording and preserving nearly every aspect of his life in voluminous diaries, notebooks, and letters. At present the greatest portion of this resource material is housed at the Henry E. Huntington Library in San Marino, California. Together with the papers of his son, Cave Jr., these make up a collection of manuscripts of some 16,000 pieces. Out of this number two diaries are perhaps best recognized.

Couts completed the first diary within a six month span between 1848 and 1849. This was a narrative of his overland march under the command of Major Lawrence P. Graham[6] from Monterrey, Mexico, to Los Angeles, where he began his tour of occupation duty in southern California. Published by the Arizona Pioneers' Historical Society in 1961 as *Hepah California! The Journal of Cave Johnson Couts from Monterrey, Nuevo Leon, Mexico to Los Angeles, California, During the Years 1848-1849*, it has become a minor classic in the realm of southwest travel memoirs.

The second diary covered Couts' involvement with the boundary survey and his escorting of an army survey party to the Colorado River from September, 1849, to December of that year. It was published in 1932 by the Zamorano Club as *From San Diego to the Colorado in 1849: The Journal and Maps of Cave J. Couts*.[7] In the interval between these two events, Couts spent several months in San Diego—initially at Mission San Luis Rey and then in Old Town. For whatever reason, the three-and-a-half pages of intermittent entries which he wrote describing this period were not published in either of the two diaries. These are the pages printed here for the first time.

The significance of this portion of Couts' diary to San Diego history can be appreciated when it is compared to the other primary accounts written in 1849.

As San Diego had become a favorite spot for those traveling to California by southern routes (around Cape Horn at the tip of South America, or traversing the isthmus of Central America) to catch steamships north or a place to stop and take on supplies, gold seekers often found time to record their impressions of the former colonial Mexican outpost of San Diego. Fortunately some of their diaries and journals survive today. For example, that of an obscure artist, H.M.T. Powell, who remained in Old Town for a short while, made sketches "of San Diego from Fort Stockton,"[10] and sold them to a variety of persons including Couts. Men like John W. Audubon,[12] youngest son of the well-known ornithologist, however, were in a greater hurry to reach the gold fields and stayed only long enough "to get provisions ready for the company" and chronicle a few brief remarks on the "beautiful" bay and the "once evidently beautiful and comfortable" Mission San Diego.[1]

21 THE GREAT POTATO FAMINE

The great influx of Irish immigrants to the United States during the mid-1800s can be attributed to the potato.

The Irish potato famine in 1845, was an unusual blight, which devastated Ireland's potato crop, the basic staple in the population, causing the majority of people to depend upon the tuber for their diet. Most Irish peasants rented small plots of land from absentee British landlords, and because an acre of potatoes could support a family for a year, it became vital to survival.

Potatoes are nutritious and easy to grow, requiring minimal labor, training or equipment. A spade is all that's required. When the blight struck, the potatoes turned slimy, black, and rotten in just days after they were dug from the ground.

A variety of causes were suspected, from static electricity to smoke bellowing from railroad locomotives, even the vapors from volcanoes. The actual cause was a fungus that had traveled from North America to Ireland.

The blight resulted in what became known as "Famine Fever," killing thousands of people suffering from cholera, dysentery, scurvy, typhus, and infestations of lice. Those trying to combat conditions reported seeing children crying with pain and looking "like skeletons, their features sharpened with hunger and their limbs wasted, so that little was left but bones."

Masses of bodies were buried without coffins only a few inches below the soil. Some 750,000 Irishmen died from the famine over the next decade to around 1855.

The British-controlled government did little to help, merely forcing hundreds of thousands into workhouses.

Within the first five years of what was known among the Irish as "The Great Hunger," the population of Ireland had been reduced by 25 percent.

Ireland wasn't the only country to be struck by the fungus, known as *Phytophthora infestans*, it reached into northern Europe, primarily Norway, causing famine in that country. A great number of Norwegians also migrated to other countries in the New World and other parts of Europe.

During the decade of the famine, more than 2 million Irishmen left their homeland, migrating to the U.S., Canada, England, and Australia.

In November 1950 – The Chinese Red army entered the Korean War crossing over from Manchuria with some 300,000 troops. They nearly surrounded more than 12,000 Allied troops at the Chosin Reservoir in far North Korea near the Manchurian border. Those Allied troops, (mostly U.S. Marines, along with U.S. Army and British troops), who fought their way back to South Korea and survived have become known as the "Frozen Chosin" because temperatures reached as low as 50 degrees below zero. A good number of those men live among us here in the North County.

22 THE SURVEY LINE THAT MARKS FOUR U.S. STATES

In 1763, two rather obscure surveyors settled a border dispute involving Delaware, Pennsylvania, and Maryland. Today, the demarcation line drawn for the map of Colonial America serves as a border for the above three states, plus West Virginia.

The names of those two surveyors have lived on through a civil war to present-day America. The survey line drawn by Charles Mason and Jeremiah Dixon is the unofficial cultural border separating the north from the southern states. The term "Dixie" came into being and has since been a term designating the southern states.

The dispute was created in 1681, by King Charles II, when he granted a colony charter to William Penn. Previously, a 1632, royal decree had granted Charles Calvert, Baron of Baltimore, the colony of Maryland.

Maryland's charter granted the land north of the entire length of the Potomac River up to the 40th parallel. Charles' Pennsylvania grant caused a problem. His grant defined Pennsylvania's southern border as identical to Maryland's northern border, but described it differently because the King relied on an inaccurate map.

The terms of the Pennsylvania grant indicated that Charles II and William Penn believed the 40th parallel would intersect the so-called "Twelve-Mile Circle" around what is today New Castle, Delaware, when in fact it falls north of the original boundaries of the City of Philadelphia, the site of which Penn had already selected for his colony's capital city.

In 1681, negotiations began to solve the problem. The next year, King Charles II proposed a compromise, which might have resolved the issue, however, it was undermined by Penn when he received the additional grant of the "Three Lower Counties" along Delaware Bay, which later became the Delaware Colony, a satellite of Pennsylvania.

Years later, in 1732, the proprietary governor of Maryland, Charles Calvert, 5th Baron of Baltimore, signed a provisional agreement with William Penn's sons, which drew a line somewhere in between and renounced the Calvert claim to Delaware. But later, Lord Baltimore claimed the document he had signed did not contain the terms he agreed to, and refused to put the agreement into effect.

In the mid-1730s, violence erupted between settlers claiming various loyalties to Maryland and Pennsylvania. The border conflict became known as Cresap's War.

Progress was made after a court ruling affirming the 1732 agreement, but the issue remained unresolved until Frederick Calvert, 6th Baron of Baltimore ceased contesting the claims on the Maryland side and accepted the earlier agreements. Maryland's border with Delaware was to be based on the "Trans-peninsular Line" and the "Twelve-Mile Circle" around New Castle. The Pennsylvania-Maryland border was defined as the line of latitude 15 miles south of the southernmost house in Philadelphia (on what is today South Street).

To settle the dispute, Penn and Calvert hired British astronomer Charles Mason and surveyor Jeremiah Dixon to survey the newly-established boundaries between the Province of Pennsylvania, the

Province of Maryland, and the Delaware Colony. It cost the Calvert family of Maryland and the Penn family of Pennsylvania an enormous amount of money to have the 244-mile border surveyed, but the two families considered it money well-spent because there was no other way of establishing land ownership between the two colonies.

After Pennsylvania abolished slavery in 1781, the western part of the colony and the Ohio River became a border between Virginia (today West Virginia), separating slave and free states. Delaware retained its slavery until the 13th Constitutional Amendment was ratified in 1865.

Today, various survey markers can be found along the four-state borders, some of private property, so owner permission is necessary to see them.

23 ROBERT E. LEE: HERO OF THE SOUTH

He spent most of his military career as a U.S. soldier. When the war between the states broke out, he was superintendent of the U.S. Military Academy (West Point). Abraham Lincoln offered him high command of the Army, but from 1862 to 1865, Robert E. Lee chose to return to his native Virginia and command the Confederate forces.

Lee was born Jan. 19, 1807, at Stratford Hall Plantation in Westmoreland County, Virginia. He was the son of the Revolutionary War's Maj. Gen. Henry "Light Horse Harry" Lee III.

One of Lee's great-grandparents, Henry Lee I, was a prominent Virginia colonist of English descent. The Lee family is one of Virginia's first families, with Richard Lee originally arriving from England in the early 1600s. Robert E. Lee's mother grew up at Shirley Plantation, one of the most elegant homes in Virginia. Lee's father "Light Horse Harry," was a not very successful tobacco planter, who suffered severe financial reverses from failed investments.

A top graduate of West Point, for more than 30 years, Robert E. Lee was an exceptional officer in the U.S. Army's combat engineer corps. He served at many posts throughout the United States, and distinguished himself during the <u>Mexican-American War</u>. He then was appointed as superintendent at West Point.

When Virginia declared its secession from the <u>Union</u> in April 1861, Lee reluctantly chose to follow his home state, despite his personal desire for the country to remain intact and despite Lincoln's offer of senior Union Army command.

In the early days of the Civil War, Lee didn't lead troops in the field. During the first year, he served as a senior military adviser to Confederate President <u>Jefferson Davis</u>. Once Lee took command of the main field army in 1862, he quickly emerged as a shrewd tactician and battlefield commander, winning most of his battles, all against far superior Union armies.

However, Lee's strategic foresight was more questionable, and both of his major offensives into the North ended in defeat. Historians have questioned Lee's aggressive tactics, which resulted in high casualties at a time when the Confederacy had a shortage of manpower. An example was the bloody battles at Gettysburg and Antietam. Union General <u>Ulysses S. Grant</u>'s campaigns bore down on the Confederacy in 1864 and 1865, and despite inflicting heavy casualties.

There was much animosity against Lee's battlefield success, so much so, that the Union Army confiscated his wife's plantation in Arlington, Va., outside of Washington, D.C., and began burying fallen soldiers in the front lawn of the mansion. Today, Lee's home still sits on a hill at the end of Arlington Cemetery, overlooking the nation's sacred national military burial grounds.

Unable to turn the war's tide, on April 9, 1865, Lee surrendered to Grant at <u>Appomattox Court House</u>. By then, Lee was supreme commander of the remaining Southern armies; other Confederate forces swiftly capitulated after his surrender. While a number of rebel pockets of resistance remained, Lee rejected a sustained insurgency against Union forces and called for reconciliation between the two sides.

It is generally believed that Lee, personally, was against slavery and openly opposed secession. After the war, he became president of what is now <u>Washington and Lee University</u>. Lee supported President <u>Andrew Johnson</u>'s program of <u>Reconstruction</u> and intersectional friendship, but he opposed the <u>radical Republican</u> proposals to give freed slaves the vote and take the vote away from ex-Confederates.

Lee urged the radical Republicans to rethink their position between the North and the South, and the reintegration of former Confederates into the nation's political life.

Since the Civil War, Lee has become the one of the great heroes of the Civil War, as his popularity has become almost mythical even in the North, especially after his death in 1870. He is buried under Lee's Chapel at Washington & Lee University.

24 ULYSSES S. GRANT
HERO OF THE CIVIL WAR

Ulysses Simpson Grant is considered the hero of the Civil War because his Union Troops outmaneuvered the Southern forces, resulting in a final victory.

Grant was known for his cigar-smoking and whiskey-drinking habits. When his heavy drinking was brought to the attention of President Abraham Lincoln, he replied: "Find out what kind he (Grant) drinks and send each one of my generals a case." Lincoln had been plagued with a series of top commanders who wouldn't pursue the enemy on a consistent basis.

Grant became an unlikely hero. Up until the Civil War, he had failed at nearly everything he tried in civilian life. Grant graduated in 1843 from the U.S. Military Academy at West Point and quit after serving in the Mexican-American War. When the Civil War began in 1861, he rejoined the U.S. Army.

Born Hiram Ulysses Grant on April 27, 1822, in Pleasant Point, Ohio, (he gave himself the middle name "Simpson," dropping "Hiram), he rose through the Army ranks and into the White House as the 18th President of the United States, twice elected (1869-77).

His successful campaign in the West, primarily winning the

Battle of Shiloh and gaining Union control of the Mississippi in the victory at Vicksburg, divided the Confederacy in half. For that feat, Lincoln finally had found a leader who would fight and appointed Grant Army Commanding General. From that point on, he worked closely with Lincoln to lead the Union Army to victory.

In 1864, Grant confronted Confederate General Robert E. Lee in a series of bloody battles, trapping Lee's army in Richmond. Grant coordinated a series of devastating campaigns in other theaters, including Gen. William T. Sherman's devastating march through Georgia. On April 9, 1865, Lee's surrender to Grant at Appomattox ended the war. Grant's military genius, and his strategies are featured in military history textbooks, but a minority of historians contend they won by overwhelming force, rather than superior strategy. As far as Lincoln was concerned, Grant was successful, no matter how he did it.

After the War, Grant led the Army's supervision of "Reconstruction" of the former Confederate states. Elected president as a Republican in 1868 and reelected in 1872, Grant stabilized the nation; he prosecuted the Ku Klux Klan, and enforced civil and voting rights laws.

After the disenfranchisement of some former Confederates, the Republicans gained majorities and African-Americans were elected to Congress and a number of important state offices.

In his second term, the Republican coalitions in the South splintered and were defeated one by one as conservative whites regained control using coercion and violence. His presidency often came under criticism for tolerating corruption and in his second term leading the nation into a severe economic depression.

Grant's Indian policy initially reduced frontier violence, but is remembered for the Great Sioux War of 1876, where Lt. Col. George Custer and his 7th Cavalry regiment were killed at the Battle of the Little Bighorn.

In 1880, Grant was unsuccessful in obtaining the nomination for a third term. Facing severe investment reversals and dying of throat cancer, he completed his memoirs, which proved a major critical and financial success. Mark Twain published Grant's best-selling autobiography, sold one copy at-a-time, "door-to-door" as there were few bookstores in those days).

Grant's death in 1885 prompted an outpouring of national unity, however, historians' evaluations of Grant's presidency were negative until the 1980s. They continue to take a dim view of Grant's economic mismanagement, despite his concern for Native Americans and enforcement of civil and voting rights.

Grant died July 23, 1885. His body was entombed in New York's Riverside Park. His funeral drew 1.5 million in attendance. Ceremonies were held in other major cities and those who eulogized Grant compared him to George Washington and Abraham Lincoln. Twelve years later his body was moved to the General Grant National Memorial, also known as "Grant's Tomb," which is the largest mausoleum in North America.

Today, Grant is a hero in most Civil War history books and his portrait graces the U.S. $50 bill.

25 THE SHORTEST TERM U.S. PRESIDENT

William Henry Harrison was, quite briefly, the ninth President of the United States, an American military officer, politician, and the first Chief Executive to die in office.

Born Feb. 9, 1773, Harrison was 68 years old when inaugurated on March 3, 1841, the oldest President to take office until Ronald Reagan. He died of pneumonia a month later on April 4, 1841. The new President had delivered his inaugural address in a steady rain. With a touch of bravado, Harrison refused an umbrella and, as a result, he quickly became ill.

It was the shortest tenure in United States Presidential history, igniting a brief constitutional crisis about succession left unanswered by the Constitution until the 1967 passage of the 25th Amendment.

Before election, Harrison gained national fame in 1811 for leading U.S. forces against combined tribes led by Tecumseh at the Battle of Tippecanoe where he earned the nickname "Old Tippecanoe."

At a time of high tensions and looming war clouds with England, many Americans blamed the British for inciting the Indian tribes to violence and supplying them with firearms. In response, Congress passed resolutions condemning the British for interfering in American domestic affairs. A few months later, the U.S. declared war against England, which became known as the War of 1812.

During a peace parley, Tecumseh had launched an impassioned plea to General Harrison, but the general was unable to understand the Indian leader's language. A Shawnee friendly to Harrison cocked his pistol from the sidelines to alert Harrison that Tecumseh's speech was leading to trouble. Some witnesses reported Tecumseh was encouraging the warriors to kill Harrison. Many of the Indians began to pull their weapons, representing a substantial threat to the general. Harrison and his officers pulled their swords and firearms, causing Tecumseh's warriors to back down.

Harrison's most notable action during the War of 1812 was in the Battle of the Thames in 1813, which caused the death of Tecumseh.

After the war, Harrison was elected to the U.S. House of Representatives, then elected to and served in the Ohio State Senate from 1819 to 1821, having lost the election for Ohio governor in 1820.

In marriage, Anna and William Harrison had 10 children. Nine lived into adulthood and one died in infancy. Anna frequently was in poor health during the marriage, primarily due to her many pregnancies. She outlived her husband by 23 years, dying at age 88 on Feb. 25, 1864.

But Harrison was less than a war hero for being a slave-owner. Reportedly, Harrison, had six children born into slavery. Four were said to be sold to a planter in La Grange, Georgia.

In 1840, Harrison was the Whig candidate against the incumbent President Martin Van Buren. Harrison was chosen over more controversial Whig members such as Henry Clay and Daniel Webster. Harrison based his campaign on his military record and on the weak U.S. economy of Van Buren, which caused the "Panic of 1837." The Whigs nicknamed him "Van Ruin."

The Whigs' campaign slogan, *"Tippecanoe and Tyler too,"* became among the most famous in American politics. On election day, Harrison won an electoral college landslide victory, though the popular vote was much closer: 53 percent to 47 percent.

Notably, William Henry Harrison was the grandfather of Benjamin Harrison, the 23rd President from 1889 to 1893.

26 CRAZY HORSE: THE NOBLE, DEFIANT NATIVE AMERICAN

In describing Crazy Horse, the famed Oglala Lakota Sioux leader, author <u>Chris Hedges</u> observed, "*There are few resistance figures in American history as noble as Crazy Horse. His ferocity of spirit remains a guiding light for all who seek lives of defiance.*"

Arguably, Crazy Horse was our most famous Native American leader. Names such as Tecumseh, Sitting Bull, Pontiac, Black Hawk, Keokuk, Geronimo and Cochise are iconic, but Crazy Horse captured the imagination the most. He was never defeated in battle.

Born circa 1840, he led a combined tribal army against the U.S. Army in 1876-77, fighting land grabs settlers and miners were taking from territories reserved exclusively for his people. The highlight was Crazy Horse's 1876 victory at the Battle at the Little Big Horn in eastern Montana.

Igniting Crazy Horse's wrath was when a company of 29 troopers entered a camp to arrest an Indian for stealing a rancher's cow. The army claimed theft, but the Indians maintained the animal wandered into the camp. It was slaughtered and the meat distributed among the people. A fight broke out and the Indians killed all of the troopers.

The unrest culminated in Crazy Horse's surprise attack on General George Crook's force of 1,000 cavalry and infantry at the Battle of Rosebud. The Indian leader led a combined tribal army of 1,500 Lakota Sioux and Cheyenne warriors. Crook's defeat prevented him from supporting Lt. Col. George Armstrong's 7th Cavalry as they began looking for Crazy Horse. A week of searching ended in a surprise attack on June 25 1876, as Crazy Horse surrounded Custer and 200-plus troopers at the Little Big Horn River. Custer and his entire unit were wiped out.

On Jan. 8, 1877, Crazy Horse's warriors fought their last major battle against the U.S. Cavalry at Wolf Mountain in the Montana Territory. After enduring starvation during a long winter, Crazy Horse surrendered to protect his followers. They went to Fort Robinson in Nebraska. What followed was an unfortunate misinterpretations of statements made by Crazy Horse.

In August 1877, officers at Camp Robinson received word the Nez Perce had broken out in Idaho and were fleeing toward Canada. When asked to join the Army against the Nez Perce, Crazy Horse objected, saying he had promised to remain at peace when he surrendered. When pressed, Crazy Horse finally agreed, saying he would fight "till all the Nez Perce were killed." His words were misinterpreted by a scout, who reported Crazy Horse had said he would "go north and fight until not a white man is left."

With the growing trouble, General Crook was ordered to stop at Fort Robinson where he was incorrectly informed Crazy Horse had said he intended to kill the general. Crook ordered Crazy Horse's arrest and departed.

On the morning of Sept. 5, 1877, Crazy Horse was escorted to Fort Robinson where he was arrested. Crazy Horse struggled with a guard and was stabbed with a bayonet. He died late that night.

The war chief's body was turned over to his elderly parents, who moved it to a location which remains unknown to this day.

No other Native American has caught the imagination of so many. Accordingly, the nation's largest mountain sculpture, begun in the early 1950s, is being carved into his image near Mount Rushmore in the Black Hills.

27 HARVARD DIDN'T WANT THEIR MONEY

During a meeting with officials of Harvard College in Cambridge, Mass., they were a relatively-unknown couple from California. They were offering several million dollars to Harvard if the college would name a facility or library after their deceased teen-aged son. Harvard turned them down. Somewhat disappointed, they returned to California and later started their own university – Stanford.

Born March 9, 1824, Leland Stanford rose to become a powerful American tycoon, industrialist, and politician. In 1851, he was a country attorney when he came to California during the Gold Rush years. He became a millionaire merchant and the chief investor of the western section of the nation's first transcontinental railroad.

Stanford was one of the four major investors in the Central Pacific Railroad, of which he was president. His partners, who also became California business tycoons, were: Charles Crocker (Crocker National Bank), Mark Hopkins (San Francisco's Mark Hopkins Hotel), and Collis P. Huntington, (San Marino's Huntington Library and Botanical Gardens, cities of Huntington Beach and Huntington Park).

Beginning in 1861, Stanford served a two-year term as

Governor of California, and later, eight years as U.S. Senator. He had tremendous power and a lasting impact on California. His detractors considered him a robber baron.

On May 10, 1869, as head of the railroad that built the western portion of the "first transcontinental railroad" over the High Sierra mountains of California, Stanford presided at the ceremonial driving of "Last (golden) Spike" at Promontory, Utah. The Central Pacific met the Union Pacific Railroad, which had been constructed west from its western terminus at Council Bluffs, Iowa and Omaha, Neb.

The Stanfords owned a palatial Sacramento mansion where their only son, Leland Stanford Jr., was born; their home on San Francisco's Nob Hill was destroyed in the 1906, earthquake; today that home site is occupied by the Stanford Court Hotel.

Stanford became a leading member of the Republican Party and was chosen as a delegate which selected U.S. presidential candidates in both 1856 (John C. Fremont) and 1860 (Abraham Lincoln). He was the first Republican Governor of California, serving two years from 1862 to 1863.

During his gubernatorial tenure, Stanford cut the state's debt in half, and advocated for the conservation of forests. He also oversaw the establishment of the California's first state normal (teacher's) school in San José, later to become San José State University. During Stanford's governorship, the term of office changed from two years to four years, taking effect in 1864, after he left office.

Stanford University was founded as a memorial to Leland Stanford, Jr., who died in 1884 of typhoid fever while on a family vacation in Italy. The Stanfords donated approximately $40-million (over $1-billion in 2015 dollars) to develop the university in Palo Alto. Stanford University's first student was Herbert Hoover, who would later become President of the United States.

Stanford died of heart failure at his home in Palo Alto, on June 21, 1893. He was buried in the family mausoleum on the Stanford campus. Jane Stanford died in 1905, in a suspected murder while vacationing in Honolulu. She had been poisoned with strychnine. The killer was never found, although it was suspected a member of her household probably was the culprit.

28 THE NEARLY FORGOTTEN PRESIDENT

His name has been the brunt of jokes by comedians for years. He's one of America's little-known Presidents, yet, Millard Fillmore held office and made important decisions in a critical time in United States history.

The 1848 Whig National Convention nominated U.S. Army Genera; Zachary Taylor (a slaveholder from Louisiana) for President. This upset supporters of Congressman Henry Clay and "Conscience Whigs" opposed to slavery in territories gained in the Mexican-American War. A group of Whig pragmatists sought to balance the ticket, and nominated Fillmore for Vice President. Fillmore came from a free state, had moderate anti-slavery views, and could help carry his populous state of New York.

With the death of President Zachary Taylor, Fillmore became the 13th President, serving from 1850 to 1853. He was the last Whig Party President.

Fillmore was a lawyer from New York State, serving as a Congressman from 1833 to 1843. He became President at the height of the slavery crisis of 1850. When the Whig Party broke up in 1854–1856, Fillmore and other conservative Whigs joined the American Party, the political arm of the anti-immigrant, anti-

Catholic "Know-Nothing" movement, though he himself was not anti-Catholic. He was the American Party candidate for President in 1856, but finished third.

During the Civil War, Fillmore denounced secession and agreed the Union must be maintained by force if necessary. He was very critical of the war policies of President Abraham Lincoln.

When Fillmore became President, the nation became embroiled in the so-called "Crisis of 1850" with the Pro-slavery Southerners demanding all of the new territories should be open to slavery. Northerners demanded complete exclusion. The recently-admitted state of Texas claimed a large part of New Mexico, and wanted the U.S. to assume their "national debt" of the former Republic of Texas. California settlers were petitioning for immediate admission as a free state. There also were slavery disputes in the District of Columbia, about the apprehension of slaves who escaped to the free Northern states, and the territorial status of newly-settled Utah.

President Taylor had stunned his fellow Southerners by urging the immediate admission of California and New Mexico as slavery-free states. Ironically, it was Fillmore, the Northerner, who supported slavery in at least part of the New Mexico territory to avoid an open break with the South.

Henry Clay constructed a compromise bill, which included provisions desired by both sides. Fillmore did not comment publicly on the merits of any of the compromise proposals.

Taking action on other controversial problems, Fillmore sent a message to Congress recommending Texas's debts be paid provided that state abandoned its claims to the New Mexico territory. Fillmore appointed Brigham Young as the first governor of the Utah Territory in 1850.

American merchants and ship owners wanted Japan "opened up" for trade and be able to put into port during emergencies without being considered as criminals by the Japanese. Fillmore dispatched Commodore Matthew C. Perry to open Japan to relations with the outside world.

Before his death, Fillmore helped to establish the University of Buffalo, as well as, a number of other Buffalo civic facilities. He died March 8, 1874.

29 JESSE JAMES: ROBIN HOOD, ROGUE, OR VICIOUS KILLER?

One of the most controversial characters in American history was the outlaw Jesse James. What makes him an enigma is that no historian has ever been able to determine his real story – the myth and legends are, well -- legendary.

Born in 1847, near the small farming community of Kearney in Clay County, Missouri, some 40 miles northeast of Kansas City, Jesse James became a bank and train robber.

The approach of the Civil War loomed large in Missouri, a border state and some 75 percent of the population was from the South or other border states. Jesse and his older brother, Frank, became Confederate guerrillas accused of atrocities committed against Union soldiers. Frank allegedly joined William C. Quantrill's guerilla raiders, but there's no evidence he took part in the infamous Lawrence, Kansas attack where more than 200 abolitionists were murdered.

Jesse first became known nationally in 1869, when he and Frank robbed a bank in Gallatin near their hometown of Kearney. They didn't get much money. Witnesses reported that Jesse shot and killed a bank clerk.

The James brothers joined Bob, Cole, and Jim Younger and continued robbing banks and stagecoaches, often joking with bystanders, then on July 21, 1873, they turned to train robbery, derailing a Rock Island passenger train, stealing approximately $3,000.

In 1874, after enduring a number of train robberies, the Adams railway express company turned to the Allan Pinkerton National Detective Agency in Chicago to stop the James-Younger gang.

On a January night in 1875, Pinkerton himself led a raid on the James family home. A firebomb was thrown into the house, killing the James brothers' mentally-disabled half-brother, Archie, plus blowing off one of the arms of Zerelda, their mother.

The gang was decimated on Sept. 7, 1876, when they attempted to rob a bank in Northfield, Minnesota. Nearly everyone in the gang was killed or captured, except Jesse and Frank. A number of townspeople saw what was happening and started shooting at the gang members, killing or wounding them in the streets.

Trying to recoup, Jesse and Frank continued robbing as far south as Mississippi and Lousiana, but by 1881, they returned to Missouri. Jesse and his wife, Zerelda, who was a cousin named after Jesse's mother, moved to St. Joseph, not far from Kearney, but Frank left for Virginia.

With his gang gone, Jesse trusted only Charley and Bob Ford. He was unaware Bob had conspired with Missouri Governor Thomas T. Crittenden to help capture Jesse in exchange for a reward. Nothing was said about Ford killing Jesse.

As the story goes, on April 3, 1882, Jesse noticed a crooked (or dusty) frame on the living room wall. While straightening it, he was shot in the back of the head by Bob Ford.

The death of Jesse James made headlines across America. In an effort to quell an outraged Missouri public, the governor later granted Frank a full pardon. Later, Bob Ford was shot and killed in Colorado.

Jesse's death was doubted by many with some reporting him

living to 101 years. He has been the subject of pulp novels and films, becoming America's Robin Hood, but what is his true story? In many ways, Jesse James was an enigma wrapped in a mystery. The truth depends upon whose telling the story. Was that picture frame crooked or dusty?

HISTORY'S BUSIEST CENTURY

30 THE GREAT WAR: CLASH OF THE VICTORIAN COUSINS

Following and understanding the history of Britain's Queen Victoria and Prince Albert, their nine children, 20 grandsons and 22 granddaughters, is daunting at best.

The marriages of the nine Victorian children created their own "United Nations." Up until the early part of the 20th century, royalty throughout Europe married off their sons and daughters to each other thinking it was a safe and prudent way to provide important alliances for diplomatic, military, economic, and social benefit. In most cases, including the marriage of Victoria and Albert, the marriages were arranged often without the two principles ever knowing or even meeting one another.

The nine Victorian children, (in order of birth), Victoria, Albert Edward (King Edward VII), Alice, Alfred, Helena, Louise, Arthur, Leopold, and Beatrice, had children, many of whom were responsible for igniting a powder keg that would plunge the world into what was deemed "The War to End All Wars."

The Victorian cousins ended up ruling Germany, Russia, Norway, Greece, Romania, Spain, and of course, Great Britain.

Victoria's and Albert's first child, Princess Victoria, was married to Prussia's (Germany) Crown Prince Frederick. From that marriage, Queen Victoria's first grandchild became the future German Emperor, Wilhelm II, the leading bad guy in WWI.

Prince Albert Edward, who, upon Victoria's death, became King Edward VII, married Denmark's Princess Alexandra. From that union came Britain's future King George V, (the grandfather of present-day Queen Elizabeth II). Also, their daughter, Maud, became queen of Norway.

Princess Alice married Louis the IV, Grand Duke of Hesse (a small duchy in Germany). They had two sons and five daughters, one of whom became Russia's Czarina Alexandra. She married Czar Nicholas II, whom, along with their family, were overthrown during the 1917 Bolshevik revolution.

The storied career of Mountbatten, youngest son of Princess Victoria and Louis Battenberg IV, is a book in itself. As Britain's Admiral of the Fleet, "Dickie" Mountbatten was the WWII Supreme Allied Commander of the Southeast Asia forces, and was the last Viceroy of India. Louie was the favorite uncle and mentor of present-day Prince Charles. Mountbatten was the uncle of Prince Phillip, husband of Queen Elizabeth II. (Prince Phillip and Queen Elizabeth II are third cousins).

(Note: During World War I, Britain's royal family changed their name from "Battenberg" to the less-German name of "Windsor."

The Royal families of Europe were a maze of Victoria's descendants. What was designed to be marriages of convenience, ensuring mutual benefit ended in a horrific World War. That tinderbox was ignited with the July 1914 assassination of Austria's Archduke Franz Ferdinand and his wife in Sarajevo, Bosnia.

The assassin was a Serbian. The Kingdom of Serbia was an ally of Russia; Bosnia was in the Austrian-Hungary Empire, an ally of

Germany. This diplomatic mess set off a crisis causing Austria-Hungary to give Serbia an "or else" ultimatum, which invoked the series of royal alliances. Within a month the First World War began.

During World War I, the primary royal heads-of-state were Queen Victoria's grandchildren: Britain's King George V, who was allied with France, as well as his cousin, Russia's Czarina Alexandra. Those three nations formed the "Allied Forces." On the other side, Cousin Wilhelm II, the Kaiser of the German Empire, was allied with Kaiser Franz Josef of the Austria-Hungary Empire, as well as the Ottoman Empire (Turkey, and what today is Iran, Saudi Arabia, Iraq, and Syria), forming the "Central Powers." The war ripped Europe apart with only Britain's monarchy surviving. The Russian revolution toppled Nicholas and Alexandra; Kaiser Wilhelm was banished to Holland; the Austria-Hungary and Ottoman empires crumbled.

Six descendants of Victoria and Albert were victims of assassination, all during the 20th century: Russia's Alexandra and her husband, Czar Nicholas II, their son, Alexei, daughters, Olga, Tatiana, Maria, and Anastasia. The last was of Louis Mountbatten killed in 1979, by the IRA.

This report is only the tip of the iceberg regarding European royal family inter-marriages. If you venture into the family lineage of Queen Victoria, be prepared to endure a mind-boggling, often confusing, family tree. It would take a sizable book to explain everything.

31 THE SAGA OF THE FORD FAMILY

If ever there was a story deserving of a Hollywood movie, the saga of the Ford family is at the top of that list.

Everyone knows Henry Ford was a pioneer in automobile manufacturing, but while he didn't invent the automobile, Ford was the first automaker to mass produce vehicles. He created the assembly line, making it possible to roll out dozens of automobiles each day. Nearly everyone in American could afford a Model T. Accordingly, cities, counties, states, and the federal government, had to build streets and highways for cars, thus connecting the population across America. People who never had been more than 25 miles from home, were free to venture 35 to 40 miles in little more than an hour.

As his empire expanded, Henry Ford became a troubled man. He was anti-Semitic and said as much in scathing editorials in his weekly newspaper distributed nationally through his dealerships. Prior to the outbreak of World War II, he was an isolationist, vehemently railing against America getting involved in any war. He made it known his successor would be Edsel, yet, to coin a phrase, never really gave his son "the keys to the car." Despite Edsel being the president of the company, Henry's constant criticisms and rejection of ideas helped drive Edsel to an early grave. Examples: Henry steadfastly believed all Americans really needed was the 1915 Model T, one of the company's biggest all-time sellers. It was Edsel who finally persuaded his father to introduce the 1927 Model A. Then Edsel went to the mat, finally convincing his father the 1932 V-8 engine was the auto power plant of the future.

When Edsel wanted to offer multiple colors on auto exteriors like other companies, Henry flatly rejected the idea declaring, "Buyers can have any color they want as long as it's black!"

There was a dark side to Henry. He was surrounded by a gang of thugs posing as "security." The "bodyguards" were led by Harry Bennett, who gained tremendous influence over the old man, coming between father and son. Henry never realized the extent of Bennett's power. In reality, he had control of the company by intimidating executives and workers and shutting Edsel out.

In 1943, Edsel died of stomach cancer, leaving the old man back in charge, but Bennett continued to control Ford. When the war started, the company was not meeting Washington's demand for aircraft, tanks, various other vehicles, and armaments. Realizing the problem, the War Department took Lt. Henry Ford II, the grandson, out of the Navy and placed him in charge of the company. One of the first decisions the young executive, (who became known as "Hank the Deuce") made was to fire Bennett and his gang of thugs.

While Henry, his son, Edsel, and three grandsons, Henry II, Benson, and William, all made historic 20th century contributions that revolutionized the American auto industry, the sweeping accomplishments of Edsel have nearly been lost to history.

Like his father, Edsel was an inventor and transportation visionary. He introduced the Mercury, and Lincoln automobiles along with countless innovations.

So, the next time you hear that low rumble of a V-8 engine,

think of Edsel.

32 THE 'REAL' FATHER OF MODERN ELECTRICITY

Nikola Tesla was born in Serbia on July 10, 1856. He was an inventor, electrical and mechanical engineer, as well as a futurist best known for his contributions in the design of the modern "alternating current" (AC) electrical system.

In 1882, Tesla began working for Thomas Edison's Continental Edison Company in France, designing and making improvements to electrical equipment.

In 1884, Tesla came to America where he was hired by Edison to work for his Edison Machine Works. Tesla's work began with simple electrical engineering and quickly progressed to solving more difficult design problems.

Tesla was offered the task of completely redesigning the Edison Company's "direct current" (DC) generators. Tesla said he could redesign Edison's inefficient motor and generators, making an improvement in both service and economy. Edison reportedly replied: "There's fifty thousand dollars in it for you if you can do it." Edison was notoriously stingy and probably didn't have that sort of money.

After months of work, Tesla fulfilled the task and inquired

about his $50,000 payment. Edison declared he was only joking.

"Tesla, you don't understand our American humor." Instead, Edison offered Tesla a $10 raise over his $18 per week salary, but Tesla refused the offer and immediately resigned.

Tesla was rightly concerned any innovation or discovery he made while under Edison's employ would be claimed by his employer. So the innovator struck out on his own, setting up laboratories and companies to develop a range of electrical devices. His <u>patented</u> AC <u>induction motor</u> and transformer were licensed by <u>George Westinghouse</u>, who also hired Tesla as a consultant.

Tesla's work in electric power development was involved in the corporate struggle between the Tesla-Westinghouse group against Edison's company, controlled by financier J.P. Morgan, making alternating current (AC) or <u>direct current</u> (DC) the power transmission standard, referred to as the "<u>War of Currents</u>."

Tesla's AC power system won out, but in reality it was a bitter victory. Westinghouse, who had control of Tesla's developments, was going broke. He had to sell Tesla's AC patents to financier Morgan, who promptly turned Edison's company into General Electric.

Bottom line: Tesla, Edison, and Westinghouse all lost out on reaping the electrifying rewards that had developed.

Tesla went on to pursue wireless lighting and electrical distribution in his high-voltage, high-frequency power experiments and made early pronouncements on the possibility of <u>wireless communication</u> with his devices.

In his lab Tesla also conducted a range of experiments with mechanical oscillators/generators, electrical discharge tubes, and early X-ray imaging. He also built a wireless-controlled boat, one of the first ever exhibited. All of this is to say that Tesla was decades ahead of everyone else in his thinking and dreaming.

Tesla was renowned for his achievements and showmanship,

eventually earning him a reputation in popular culture as a "Mad Scientist." His patents earned him a considerable amount of money, much of which was used to finance his own projects with varying degrees of success. He lived most of his life in a series of New York hotels.

Tesla died on Jan. 7, 1943. His work fell into relative obscurity after his death, but in his honor, the 1960 General Conference on Weights and Measures named the SI unit of magnetic flux density the "Tesla."

Tesla's name and memory has experienced a resurgence in interest in popular culture since the 1990's. Today, the leading all-electric automobile company is called "Tesla Motors." The car is considered one of the top luxury vehicles in the world.

33 JOSEPH PULITZER: MAN BEHIND THE 'PRIZES'

Most people today have heard of the coveted "Pulitzer Prizes," but few know what they are is or for whom they are was named.

The Prizes are named for Joseph Pulitzer, who was born in 1847 in Hungary. He became one of America's most famous and successful newspaper publishers, starting with the St. Louis Post-Dispatch, and later the New York World.

In the 1890's, the fierce competition between *The New York World* and William Randolph Hearst's *New York Journal* caused both to use caustic editorializing, known as "yellow journalism." Pulitzer opened the way to mass-circulation newspapers that appealed to readers by offering a multiple taste in news, entertainment, and advertising.

Pulitzer joined the Republican Party through which he was able to land a reporting job for the St. Louis *Westliche Post.*

When GOP leaders needed a candidate to fill a vacancy in the State Legislature, they settled on Pulitzer, forgetting he was only 22 - three years under the minimum age. However, his chief Democratic opponent was ineligible because he had served in the Confederate army. Pulitzer won by a 209-147 vote.

His age was not made an issue and was seated as a Missouri state representative beginning in 1870. Pulitzer lived in Jefferson City for only two years, all while keeping his reporting job for the Westliche Post.

In 1872, Pulitzer was a delegate to the Cincinnati convention of the Liberal Republican Party which nominated Horace Greeley for the presidency. However, the attempt at electing Greeley as president failed, the party collapsed.

Pulitzer, disillusioned with the corruption in the Republican Party, switched to the Democratic Party. In 1880, he was a delegate to the Democratic national convention and a member of its platform committee from Missouri.

In 1883, Pulitzer, by now a wealthy man, purchased the New York World from Jay Gould for $346,000, and began emphasizing human-interest stories, scandal, and sensationalism.

In 1895, Pulitzer introduced the popular *Yellow Kid* comic strip, the first to be printed in color, which was used for editorial comment instead of mere humor.

In 1895, Hearst purchased the rival New York Journal from Pulitzer's brother, Albert, then the two embarked on a circulation war. This competition with Hearst, particularly the coverage before and during the Spanish-American War, linked Pulitzer's name with "yellow journalism" because of the caustic editorializing in the *Yellow Kid* comic strip. Historians point to the combative journalism between Hearst and Pulitzer, arguably, as one of the primary causes for the Spanish-American War.

The two publishers prodded President McKinley toward war and when the USS Maine was sunk in Havana Harbor, Hearst and Pulitzer started a war of words and pictures of their own.

Pulitzer put great stock in his reporting staff. He was once asked "… why it is that you always speak so kindly of reporters and so severely of all editors?"

"Well", Pulitzer replied, "I suppose it is because every reporter is a hope, and every editor is a disappointment."

Today, his name is kept alive with the Pulitzer Prizes, which were established in 1917, through a grant to Columbia University. The prizes are given annually to award achievements in journalism and photography, as well as literature, history, poetry, music and drama.

Right before he died in 1911, Pulitzer founded the Columbia School of Journalism with a philanthropic bequest, which was opened in 1912.

34 HEARST: FATHER OF 'YELLOW JOURNALISM'

One of America's most powerful, controversial, and hated tycoons was William Randolph Hearst. He was an American newspaper and magazine publisher, who built the nation's largest chain and whose methods profoundly influenced American journalism.

William R. Hearst was born in San Francisco in 1863, to millionaire goldmine owner and U.S. senator George Hearst and his wife, Phoebe.

After being kicked out of Harvard, Hearst took control of *The San Francisco Examiner* from his father, who owned the newspaper as payment for a debt.

Later moving to New York City, Hearst acquired *The Journal* and began a long, bitter circulation war with Joseph Pulitzer's *New York World*. This led to the creation of the term "yellow journalism," which were sensationalized stories of dubious validity.

Hearst was both lucky and unlucky when he entered politics. He was twice elected as a Democrat to the U.S. House of Representatives, but twice ran unsuccessfully for Mayor of New York City, as well as, for both governor and lieutenant governor of

New York.   However, Hearst exercised enormous political influence, and was blamed for leading the United States into the Spanish-American War.

Hearst acquired the best press equipment and the most talented writers of the time, including Ambrose Bierce, Mark Twain, and Jack London.

The *Journal's* daily circulation would routinely climb above 1 million after the 1898 sinking of the *USS Maine,* and America's entry into the Spanish-American War, dubbed "The *Journal's* War" due to the paper's immense influence in provoking American outrage against Spain's brutality against Cubans.

While the "yellow press" did not directly cause America's war with Spain, Hearst's and other papers did inflame public opinion to a fever pitch, which was a major influence in President William McKinley's decision to go to war with Spain.

By the mid-1920s, Hearst had 28 newspapers nationwide, but the economic collapse of the Great Depression and the vast over-extension of his empire cost him control of his holdings.

In 1937, Hearst Corporation faced a court-mandated bankruptcy. From that point, Hearst was reduced to merely being another employee.

Hearst died in 1951, but his name again became prominent in 1974, when his granddaughter, Patricia "Patty" Hearst, was kidnapped by and then joining the Symbionese Liberation Army. She is the daughter of Hearst's fourth son, Randolph Hearst.

One of Hollywood's most influential movies was Orson Welles's 1941 film *Citizen Kane,* which was loosely based on parts of Hearst's life. He was enraged at the idea of *Citizen Kane* being a thinly disguised and very unflattering portrait of him. Hearst used all his resources and influence in an unsuccessful attempt to prevent the film from being released - all without his ever seeing it. Welles and the movie studio, RKO, resisted Hearst's pressure, but Welles and his Hollywood friends succeeded in getting theater chains to limit their bookings of the film, resulting in mediocre box-office numbers and seriously harming Welles's career.

HBO offered a fictionalized version of Hearst in its film, *RKO 281.*

His mansion, Hearst Castle near San Simeon, was donated in 1957, by the Hearst Corporation to the State of California, and is now a state historical monument and a U.S. National Historic Landmark.

The Hearst Corporation continues to this day as a large, privately held media conglomerate based in New York City.

35 THE CURMUDGEON OF
THE AMERICAN PRESS

Henry Louis "H. L." Mencken was a journalist, essayist, editor, satirist, critic of life and culture of American, as well as, a scholar of American English.

Known as the "*Sage of Baltimore,*" Mencken was one of the most influential American writers and prose stylists of the first half of the 20th century.

Born in 1880, Mencken was the son of a cigar factory owner. When he was nine years old, he read Mark Twain's *Huckleberry Finn*, which he later described as "the most stupendous event in my life."

At age 15, he graduated as valedictorian from the Baltimore Polytechnic Institute. In early 1898, he took a class in writing at the Cosmopolitan University, the extent of his formal education in journalism, or any other subject. He applied in February 1899 to the Morning Herald newspaper and was hired on as a full-time reporter.

After six years at the Herald, Mencken then moved to *The Evening Sun* where he worked until 1948.

Mencken became noted throughout America for his editorial

opinion. He co-founded and edited *The American Mercury*, which developed a national circulation.

In 1925, Mencken covered the Scopes "Monkey" Trial in Dayton, Tennessee, writing scathing syndicated columns mocking the anti-evolution fundamentalists, especially William Jennings Bryan. The play and movie "*Inherit the Wind*" is a fictionalized account of the trial.

In 1926, Mencken followed with great interest the Los Angeles grand jury inquiry into the famous evangelist Aimee Semple McPherson. She was accused of faking her kidnapping. Mencken didn't continue his previous pattern of anti-fundamentalist articles, but came to her defense.

In 1930, Mencken married German-American Sara Haardt, a professor of English and 18 years his junior. The union was notable because Mencken once called marriage "... the end of hope." He justified his marriage by saying, "The Holy Spirit informed and inspired me. Like all other infidels, I am superstitious and always follow hunches ... this one seemed to be a superb one." But after five years, his wife developed tuberculosis and died leaving Mencken grief-stricken.

During the Great Depression, Mencken did not support President Roosevelt which cost him much popularity. He also had strong reservations regarding U.S. participation in World War II, though he considered Adolf Hitler and the Nazis "ignorant thugs."

Mencken suffered a stroke in 1948, leaving him fully conscious but nearly unable to read or write, and able to speak only with difficulty. During the last year of his life, his friend and biographer William Manchester read to him daily. Mencken died Jan. 29, 1956, buried in Baltimore.

An example of Mencken's controversial-style of editorializing can be found in a July 26, 1920 edition of *The Baltimore Sun*:

"As democracy is perfected, the office of the President represents, more and more closely, the inner soul of the people. On some great and glorious day, the plain folks of the land will

reach their heart's desire at last and the White House will be occupied by a downright fool and complete narcissistic moron."

Though it isn't on his tombstone, Mencken wrote his own epitaph: "If, after I depart this vale, you ever remember me and have thought to please my ghost, forgive some sinner and wink your eye at some homely girl."

36 'LUCKY LINDY' – 'THE LONE EAGLE'

Charles Augustus Lindbergh, born Feb. 4, 1902, was an American aviator, author, inventor, explorer, and social activist. He was most famous for his 1927 historic non-stop flight across the Atlantic from New York to Paris.

He took off May 20, from Roosevelt Field on Long Island, landing nearly 3,000 miles later at Le Bourget Field in Paris. Lindbergh was flying a specially-designed mono-plane built by San Diego's Ryan Aircraft. As a result of this flight, Lindbergh was the first person in history to be in New York one day and Paris the next.

Lindbergh, a U.S. Army Air Corps Reserve officer, also was awarded the nation's highest military decoration, the Medal of Honor, for his historic, record-breaking feat.

During the late '20s and through the 1930s, Lindbergh was the most popular man in America – possibly the world. Lindbergh used his fame to promote the development of both commercial aviation and Air Mail services in the United States and the Americas. In March 1932, his infant first-born son, Charles, Jr., was kidnapped and murdered in what was soon dubbed the "Crime of the Century." It was described by journalist H.L. Mencken, as

"...the biggest story since the resurrection." The kidnapping eventually led to the Lindbergh family's being "driven into voluntary exile" in Europe, to which they sailed in secrecy from New York under assumed names in late December 1935. In order to seek a safe, secluded home away from the wild public hysteria. Charles and Anne Lindbergh returned to the United States in April 1939.

Before the United States formally entered World War II, in December 1941, Lindbergh had been an outspoken advocate of keeping the U.S. out of the world conflict, as had his father, U.S. Rep. Charles August Lindbergh, Republican-Minn., during World War I. Before Pearl Harbor, in apparent protest, "The Lone Eagle" had resigned his Army Air Corps colonel's commission.

Although Lindbergh was a vocal leader in the anti-war America First movement, he nevertheless strongly supported the war effort after Pearl Harbor. He flew 50 combat missions in the Pacific Theater of World War II as a civilian consultant, though President Franklin D. Roosevelt had refused to reinstate his Army Air Corps colonel's commission of which "The Lone Eagle" had resigned.

However, historians speculate just how serious Lindbergh was concerning his America First advocacy. Years after his death, classified documents were uncovered that indicated Lindbergh had made a number of trips to Nazi Germany, acting as a secret agent for the U.S. War Department. While he was invited by Germany to tour their aircraft manufacturing facilities and to see the new Luftwaffe's air armada, reportedly, Lindbergh was taking careful notes and reporting back to the Army Air Corps about the Nazi buildup.

There was more discovered about the famed airman's private life after his 1974 death. A German biography revealed Lindbergh was quite unlike his clean-cut, shy Boy Scout image. He had fathered no less than seven children to three secret European mistresses.

In July 2003, some 29 years after Lindbergh's 1974 death, one of the largest national daily newspapers in Germany reported he had fathered three out-of-wedlock children by a German hat maker Brigitte Hesshaimer. Two years later it was further revealed Lindbergh had fathered four other out-of-wedlock children with two other mistresses in Germany and Switzerland. All seven children had been born between 1958 and 1967. Though he visited yearly each of his "families," none of the European children discovered the identity of their father until after his death on Aug. 26, 1974.

In his later years, Lindbergh was a prolific prize-winning author, international explorer, inventor, and environmentalist. His grave is near the Lindbergh family home at Hana on the Hawaiian island of Maui.

37 THE FATHER OF THE AMERICAN AIR FORCE

Aviation pioneer Billy Mitchell correctly predicted what lay ahead in 20th century warfare, but at great personal cost. As early as 1906, Billy Mitchell predicted the strategic implementation of future wars would take place in the air, not on the ground.

William "Billy" Mitchell, born Dec. 29, 1879, was an Army general who today is regarded the father of the United States Air Force.

In March 1912, Mitchell toured battlefields of the Russo-Japanese War and concluded that war with Japan would be a reality.

After World War I, Mitchell began advocating for an increase in air power. One of the problems he had was "the war to end all wars" had just been fought and few really believed in any future conflict.

Recognized as one of the top combat airmen of "The Great War," Mitchell was probably the best-known American in Europe. He was awarded the Distinguished Service Cross and the Distinguished Service Medal.

After the war, Mitchell began advocating that bombers could

sink battleships. While he would prove his theory, it was the beginning of Mitchell's undoing because few in either the Army or Navy shared his vision.

In February 1921, a bombing demonstration using captured German ships was reluctantly agreed to by the Navy. Mitchell had infuriated the Navy by claiming he could sink ships "under war conditions," and boasted he could prove it if he were permitted to bomb and sink captured German battleships. The demonstration was a success.

In 1923, Mitchell repeated the bombing tests with the same results on three obsolete American battleships USS Alabama, USS Virginia and USS New Jersey. President Harding and Navy officials were angry because the demonstration showed U.S. Naval weakness.

Mitchell's bombing tests caused budgets to be redrawn for further air development and forced the Navy to look more closely at the possibilities of Naval airpower. One of his predictions: There would be a future surprise attack on the Hawaiian Islands by Japan.

But Mitchell was an embarrassment to both military and civilian leaders. Accordingly, in October 1925, he was court-martialed for "insubordination" because he accused Army and Navy leaders of having an "almost treasonable administration of the national defense" by investing in battleships instead of aircraft carriers.

The court martial lasted for seven weeks. The youngest of the 12 judges was Major General Douglas MacArthur, who voted for acquittal, described sitting as a judge on Mitchell's court-martial as "one of the most distasteful orders I ever received." However, the majority found him "guilty of all specifications of the charges." The court suspended Mitchell from active duty for five years without pay, which President Coolidge later amended to half-pay.

MacArthur said afterward, "a senior officer should not be silenced for being at variance with his superiors in rank and with accepted doctrine." It was a stance that would prove to be the general's undoing decades later.

Shortly after the trial, Mitchell resigned and spent the rest of his life writing and preaching air power. He received many honors, albeit after his death on Feb. 19, 1936.

President Franklin D. Roosevelt commissioned him a Major General. He also is the only individual for whom a military aircraft, the North American B-25 Mitchell bomber, is named. The twin-engine bomber was used on the heroic Doolittle raid over Tokyo six months after the Pearl Harbor attack.

In Air Force circles Mitchell is regarded today as a hero, legend, and the Father of the U.S. Air Power.

38 AMERICA'S 1ST FLYING ACE: EDDIE RICKENBACKER

He quit school in the 7th grade; he was fascinated by machines; joined the U.S. Army as a mechanic; taught himself how to fly and became an "ace" in less than 30 days to become America's most successful fighter pilot.

This unusual man became a champion race car driver and auto designer, a government consultant on military affairs, was adrift at sea for 24 days, clashed with President Franklin Roosevelt over air mail, and headed up a major airline. These are but a few exploits in the life of Eddie Rickenbacker.

He was born Edward Rickenbacher Oct. 8, 1890, in Columbus, Ohio to Swiss German-speaking immigrants. When World War I broke out, he exchanged the "h" for a "k" to sound less German.

At age 13, Rickenbacker's schooling ended after the 1904 death of his father. The youngster found odd jobs and enrolled in a mechanical engineering correspondence course. He was especially fascinated with automobiles.

As a race car driver, Rickenbacker competed in the Indianapolis 500 four times earning the nickname, "Fast Eddie."

In 1916, Rickenbacker traveled to London to develop a race car, but because of his name, he was a suspected spy.

In 1917, the United States declared war on Germany and Rickenbacker enlisted in the U.S. Army. He was promoted to Sergeant First Class because of his mechanical abilities and assigned to the U.S. Air Service's pursuit training facility where he learned to fly during his spare time.

When he convinced senior officers of his flying abilities, Rickenbacker was placed in the famed 94th Aero Squadron, informally known as the "Hat-in-the-Ring" Squadron. In his first month in combat he shot down five enemy planes and was awarded the French Croix de Guerre for his victories. The next day he scored his sixth victory. He soon was commanding the squadron.

In 1931, Rickenbacker was belatedly awarded the Medal of Honor by President Herbert Hoover for his 26 aerial victories – the most by any American pilot during World War I.

In 1927, Rickenbacker bought the Indianapolis Motor Speedway, which he operated for 15 years. In 1942, Rickenbacker closed the Speedway due to World War II, and sold it in 1945.

Rickenbacker was adamantly opposed to President Franklin Roosevelt's New Deal policies. The President ordered NBC Radio not to allow him to broadcast opinions critical of Roosevelt's policies. Rickenbacker had harshly denounced the President's taking existing mail contracts from civilian air carriers to have Army Air Corps pilots carry the air mail.

In 1938, Rickenbacker bought Eastern Airlines from General Motors for $3.5 million.

During the 1930s, he helped develop new aircraft designs and bought the new four-engine Lockheed Constellation and Douglas DC-4 airliners. In 1941, Rickenbacker was a passenger on a DC-3 airliner that crashed near Atlanta. He suffered serious injuries, being soaked in fuel, immobile, and trapped in the wreckage.

One of Rickenbacker's most famous near-death experiences occurred in 1942 on a tour of air bases in the Pacific. Off course,

Rickenbacker's B-17 ran out of fuel, forcing the crew to ditch in a remote part of the Pacific. For 24 days, the crew drifted. Their food ran out after three days and once again, the nation's news media reported Rickenbacker was dead. A U.S. Navy patrol floatplane finally rescued them. The mishap inspired Rickenbacker to help develop improved navigational instruments and better survival gear.

At age 83, Captain Rickenbacker suffered from pneumonia and died on July 23, 1973 in Zürich, Switzerland. Throughout his eventful life, Rickenbacker was responsible for hundreds of aviation, as well as, mechanical innovations, and was one of history's most intriguing character's.

39 THE GREAT SAGE OF MIDDLE AMERICA

William Allen White was a renowned American newspaper editor, politician, author, leader of the Progressive movement, and an important spokesman for Middle America.

Born on Jan. 29, 1868, in Emporia, Kansas, White attended the College of Emporia and the University of Kansas. In 1892 started work as an editorial writer at The Kansas City Star. Three years later White bought the Emporia Gazette for $3,000.

He developed a friendship with President Theodore Roosevelt in the 1890s that lasted until Roosevelt's death in 1919. He helped Roosevelt form the Progressive (Bull-Moose) Party in 1912, in opposition to the conservative forces surrounding incumbent Republican President William Howard Taft.

With his warm sense of humor, articulate editorial pen, and common-sense approach to life, White soon became known throughout the nation as the outspoken country editor. His Gazette editorials were widely reprinted; he wrote syndicated stories on politics; and he published many books, including biographies of Woodrow Wilson and Calvin Coolidge.

White was a reporter at the post World War I Treaty of Versailles Conference in 1919 and a strong supporter of Woodrow

Wilson's proposal for the League of Nations. The League went into operation but the U.S. never joined. During the 1920s, White was critical of both the isolationism and the conservatism of the Republican Party.

In 1924, angered by the emergence of the Ku Klux Klan in the state, he made an unsuccessful run for Kansas Governor.

In the 1936, he was an early supporter of the Republican presidential nominees, Alf Landon of Kansas, and Wendell Willkie in 1940. However, White was on the liberal wing of the Republican Party and wrote many editorials praising the New Deal of President Franklin D. Roosevelt.

White won a 1923 Pulitzer Prize for his editorial "*To an Anxious Friend*," published July 27, 1922. In his novels and short stories, White developed his idea of the small town as a metaphor for understanding social change and for preaching the necessity of community.

White opposed chain stores and mail-order firms as a threat to the business owner on Middle America's small town Main Street. The Great Depression shook his faith in a cooperative, selfless, middle-class America. White concluded that democracy inevitably lacked direction. He felt President Roosevelt's New Deal during the 1930's was "baffling."

The last quarter century of White's life was spent as an unofficial national spokesman for Middle America. This led President Franklin Roosevelt to ask White to help generate public support for the Allied nations prior to America's entry into World War II.

Sometimes referred to as the "Sage of Emporia," he continued to write editorials for the Gazette until his death in 1944. He also was a founding editor of the Book of the Month Club along with longtime friend Dorothy Canfield.

White visited six of the seven continents at least once in his long life. Due to his fame and success, he received 10 honorary degrees from universities, including one from Harvard.

The paper continues as a family-run publication, headed by White's great-grandson, Christopher White Walker.

40 ONE OF OUR WORST PRESIDENTS

Warren Gamaliel Harding was the 29th President of the United States, serving from March 4, 1921 until his death on Aug. 2, 1923.

Although Harding died one of the most popular presidents in history to that point, the subsequent exposure of scandals that took place during his tenure -- such as the infamous Teapot Dome scandal -- eroded his popularity. In historical rankings of the U.S. Presidents, Harding has been rated among the worst.

Historians generally agree that if Harding was guilty of anything it was poor judgment of character and choice of appointments. He famously took care of his friends, but many of them were either unqualified for their positions or took illegal advantage of their office.

Harding was born in Blooming Grove, Ohio, Nov. 2, 1865. Except when political service took him elsewhere, he lived in rural Ohio all of his life. When not yet 20 years of age, he settled in Marion and bought the failing *The Marion Star* newspaper, building it into a successful publication.

In 1899, he was elected to the Ohio State Senate, and after four years in office successfully ran for Lieutenant Governor. He was defeated for governor in 1910, but four years later, Harding was elected to the U.S. Senate.

In 1920, when Harding ran for the Republican nomination for president, he was considered an "also-ran" with little chance of success. The leading candidates could not gain a majority in order to secure the GOP nomination, leaving the convention deadlocked. Harding's support gradually grew until he was nominated on the 10th ballot. Harding conducted a "front porch campaign" from his home in Marion, allowing supporters to come to him. Running on a theme of "return to normalcy," Harding was victorious over Democrat James M. Cox and Socialist Party candidate Eugene Debs. Harding became the first sitting U.S. senator to be elected president.

Harding preferred a low-key inauguration without the customary parade celebration. He was sworn in as President on March 4, 1921, in the presence of his wife and father. There was a brief reception at the White House where he gave a short inaugural address.

"Our most dangerous tendency is to expect too much from the government and at the same time do too little for it," he said.

Harding appointed a number of well-regarded figures to his cabinet, including Andrew Mellon as Treasury Secretary; Herbert Hoover as Secretary of Commerce; and Charles Hughes as Secretary of State.

A major foreign policy achievement came with the Washington Naval Conference of 1921–1922, in which the world's major naval powers agreed on a naval limitations program that lasted for 10 years. Harding's success was overshadowed by two of his cabinet, Interior Secretary Albert Fall and Attorney General Harry Daugherty, who were implicated in corruption.

The two Harding cabinet appointees who darkened the reputation of his administration for their involvement in scandal were Harding's Senate friend, Albert B. Fall of New Mexico, the Interior Secretary, and Daugherty, who became Attorney General.

Fall was a Western rancher and former miner, and was pro-development. He was opposed by conservationists such as Gifford Pinchot, who wrote, "It would have been possible to pick a worse man for Secretary of the Interior, but not altogether easy."

Harding appointed a number of friends and acquaintances to federal positions and served competently, while some of Harding's friends, who were dubbed the "Ohio Gang," proved corrupt.

Most of the scandals that marred the reputation of Harding's administration did not emerge until after his death.

The most memorable of the scandals involved the U.S. Naval oil reserves at Tea Pot Dome in Wyoming. Teapot Dome was one of three reserves set aside for the use by the Navy in a national emergency. There was a longstanding argument that those reserves should be developed. Harding signed an executive order transferring the reserves from the Navy Department to the Department of Interior.

Most of the scandals did not fully emerge until after Harding's death, but nonetheless, greatly damaged his reputation in history. Harding died of heart disease in San Francisco while on a western speaking tour; he was succeeded by his vice president, Calvin Coolidge, who would go on to be elected President in his own right after completing Harding's term.

41 THE OWENS VALLEY WAR

Over the years, there has been much fighting within the state of California over gold, land, oil, but nothing like the clashes over water rights. California is a "have and have not" state – half of the state has water, the other is always in need.

One of the most memorable of the water wars were the many disputes between Los Angeles and residents of the Owens Valley located in the eastern part of the state.

In the late 1800's, the city's growth demanded more water. Los Angeles officials discovered much-needed water could be brought by aqueduct from the Owens Valley. The aqueduct construction was begun in 1913, overseen by William Mulholland, an engineer who worked on the Panama Canal. Unfortunately the Owens Valley water rights for Los Angeles were acquired through political maneuvering, in-fighting and a series of outright lies to Owens Valley landowners.

By the 1920's, enough water had been diverted from the Owens Valley that growing crops became so difficult that the farmers tried to destroy the aqueduct. But the attempt was foiled and Los Angeles kept the water flowing. By 1926, Owens Lake had been nearly drained, leaving the valley completely dry.

In 1941, Los Angeles diverted water via the aqueduct that previously fed Mono Lake, which is north of Owens Valley. Between 1979 and 1994, the Mono Lake Committee brought successful lawsuits against Los Angeles, forcing the city to stop taking water from around Mono Lake.

Aside from all of the early legal wrangling, the skullduggery continued. Mulholland was assisted by Fredrick Eaton, an official with the Los Angeles City Water Company.

Beginning in 1902, Eaton used less-than-ethical tactics to get water rights for Los Angeles. A key U.S. Reclamation official, Joseph Lippincott, became a close associate of Eaton, giving Los Angeles officials inside access to the government's plans. He advised the city the best way to take the water rights from the Owens Valley.

In 1907, Eaton solidified the deal by convincing President Theodore Roosevelt the water from the Owens River would be more beneficial to Los Angeles than to Owens Valley.

To make sure his efforts for the city were ensured, Eaton bought a ranch in the Owens Valley, and turned over all his ranch's water rights free-of-charge to the City of Los Angeles.

Some historians say Eaton was devious; others say he was a shrewd businessman. Defenders say at the time, Los Angeles didn't have the money to buy Eaton's water rights and he was just being a good citizen. Later, a bond election paid Eaton for the rights, but he always denied any deception on his part.

Mulholland reportedly misled Los Angeles as early as 1905. He understated the amount of water available for the city and misled Owens Valley residents saying the city would use only "unused flows." But, all of the water was used to supply the San Fernando Valley, which flowed into the Los Angeles River, creating a large supply for the city.

To add even more pressure on Owens Valley, a second aqueduct was built in 1970,

In 1991, Los Angeles and Inyo County signed a long-term

water agreement requiring the pumping to be better managed. By 1994, most of the litigation had been settled with Los Angeles required to release water back into Mono Lake to raise the level and restore the ecosystem.

The 1974 Jack Nicholson film, "Chinatown," was partially based upon the Owens Valley wars.

42 THE TEAPOT DOME SCANDAL

Most of us have heard of the "Teapot Dome" scandal, but what was it, where was it, and what did it involve?

Teapot Dome was a scandal over oil leases that occurred in President Warren G. Harding's administration during the early 1920s. It was a decade-long affair that made countless national headlines.

Teapot Dome is an oil field in Natrona County, Wyoming. The scandal also involved the Elk Hills oil field in Kern County, California.

In the early 20th century, the U.S. Navy began converting warships from coal to oil fuel. To ensure the Navy would always have enough fuel available in case of war, in 1912, President Howard Taft designated Teapot Dome and Elk Hills as Naval oil reserve fields.

In 1921, at the urging of Interior Secretary Albert Fall, President Harding issued an executive order transferring the two oil fields from the Navy Department to the Interior Department.

Then in 1922, Fall issued a lease on the Teapot Dome oil field to Harry F. Sinclair, founder of Sinclair Oil. Fall also issued a lease on the Elk Hills reserve to legendary California oil man

Edward L. Doheny. Both leases were issued without competitive bidding. They were deemed legal under the Mineral Leasing Act of 1920.

The lease terms were very favorable to the oil companies. Fall secretly received a $100,000 interest-free loan from Doheny (about $1.5 million in today's money). He also received gifts from both Doheny and Sinclair totaling more than $400,000 ($5.5 million in today's money).

Obviously, it was the loan and gifts that were illegal. Fall attempted to keep his private dealings with Doheny and Sinclair a secret, however, the sudden improvement in his standard of living caused concern.

A complaint about the Teapot Dome lease by a small Wyoming oil producer triggered an investigation. By 1924, no evidence of wrongdoing had been uncovered, but the last-minute discovery of Fall's acceptance of money was his undoing. Investigators uncovered critical evidence that Fall had forgotten to cover up: Doheny's $100,000 loan.

The scandal broke wide open, triggering a number of civil and criminal suites. In 1927 the Supreme Court ruled the oil leases had been fraudulently obtained. The Court invalidated both the Elk Hills and Teapot Dome leases. The reserves were returned to the Navy Department.

In 1929, Secretary Fall was found guilty of bribery, fined $100,000 and sentenced to one year in prison, making him the first Presidential cabinet member to go to prison for his actions in office.

Sinclair, who refused to cooperate with investigators, was charged with contempt, fined $100,000, and received a short sentence of six months for jury tampering. Doheny was acquitted of bribery in 1930.

One of the most significant outcomes of the scandal was a Supreme Court ruling explicitly giving Congress the power to compel testimony. For those of us today who wonder just how much power the Congress has when calling people to testify, that high-court ruling speaks volumes.

Teapot Dome was one of the primary scandals that, historically, has saddled President Harding's legacy as having a corrupt administration.

43 1939: IT'S STILL THE BEST MOVIE YEAR

While movie buffs all have their favorite movie(s), few will argue that 1939 produced a string of films unrivaled in any other year and that will last forever as "classic."

It was the end of a decade filled with "feel good" movies, which helped to take the sting out of the Great Depression. Hollywood outdid itself that year, producing films that have entertained every generation since. It was the year the stars shone brightly.

The reading public was fixated on Margaret Mitchell's best-selling novel, "Gone With The Wind." Accordingly, there was a great hue and cry to see that Civil War epic on screen. Producer David O. Selznick did not disappoint. He cast Hollywood most popular leading man, Clark Gable, and newcomer Vivian Leigh, as the lead actors. While it won "Best Picture" at the Oscars, Gable lost out to Robert Donat for his role in "Good-bye Mr. Chips." Leigh surprised everyone by beating out four other leading ladies for her memorable role of Scarlet O'Hara.

In addition to "Gone With The Wind," there were too many great 1939 films to mention here, but the nominated "losers" of the Best Picture Oscar that year were: "Dark Victory," "Good-bye Mr. Chips," "Dark Victory," "Love Affair," "Mr. Smith Goes to

Washington," "Ninotchka," "Of Mice and Men," "Stagecoach," "Wuthering Heights," and, of course, "The Wizard of Oz."

It was a formidable list of actors vying for top honors in their respective roles. The cast of "Wind" was enough to compete against: with Gable, Leigh, Lesley Howard, Olivia de Haviland, and Hattie McDaniel, who won for Best Support Actress. She was the first of her race to be recognized with an Oscar. How do you vote against James Stewart as "Mr. Smith," Mickey Rooney for "Babe in Arms, and Laurence Olivier in "Wuthering Heights?"

And, then there was Greer Garson in "Mr. Chips," Irene Dunne in "Love Affair," Bette Davis in "Dark Victory," and Greta Garbo for "Ninotchka."

John Ford's "Stagecoach" was an important film because it made John Wayne a top box office star for the next 40 years until his death in 1979. Claire Trevor was his leading lady, who turned in a stellar performance. And, don't forget shady John Carradine and cavalry officer Tim Holt. Thomas Mitchell won Best Supporting Actor for his role as the drunken doctor aboard the "Stagecoach."

The 12th Academy Awards gave Walt Disney his eighth (in a row) Oscar for "The Ugly Duckling" in the animated feature category. Down through the years, Disney and costume designer Edith Head probably won more gold statuettes than any other in their category.

While "Gone With The Wind" swept most of the Oscars, "Stagecoach" won for Best Musical Score, "Wizard of Oz" for Original Score and Best Song, (Over The Rainbow).

This list could go on and on telling Hollywood's story for 1939, but it should whet the interest of film buffs to look into that year's film history.

In the meantime, Olivia de Haviland, who was nominated for Best Support Actress in "Gone With The Wind," is the only actor still living from that epic drama – probably of all of the 1939 films.

44 A SELF-MADE IOWA BOY

Herbert Clark Hoover was the 31st President of the United States (1929–1933). He was born to a Quaker family Aug. 10, 1874, and was a professional mining engineer.

Hoover achieved American and international prominence in humanitarian relief efforts in war-time Belgium, and served as head of the U.S. Food Administration during World War I.

As the United States Secretary of Commerce in the 1920s under Presidents Warren G. Harding and Calvin Coolidge, Hoover promoted partnerships between government and business under the rubric "economic modernization".

In the presidential election of 1928, Hoover easily won the Republican nomination, despite having no elected-office experience. Hoover is the most recent cabinet secretary to be elected President of the United States, as well as one of only two Presidents (along with William Howard Taft) elected without electoral experience or high military rank. President Calvin Coolidge had famously asserted that "The business of America is business," and "pro-business" policies fostered an economic bubble that peaked in America in 1929, facilitating a landslide victory for Hoover over Democrat Al Smith.

Hoover, a globally experienced engineer, believed strongly in the "Efficiency Movement," which held that the government and the economy were riddled with inefficiency and waste, and could be improved by experts who could identify the problems and solve them.

Hoover also believed in the importance of volunteerism and of the role of individuals in society and the economy. Hoover, who had made a small fortune in mining, was the first of two Presidents to redistribute their salary (President Kennedy was the other; he donated all his paychecks to charity).

When the Wall Street Crash of 1929 struck less than eight months after he took office, Hoover tried to combat the ensuing Great Depression with moderate government public works projects such as the Hoover Dam. Unfortunately, the record tariffs imbedded in the Smoot-Hawley Tariff and aggressive increases in the top tax bracket from 25 percent to 63 percent, coupled with increases in corporate taxes, yielded a "balanced budget" in 1933, but seriously hindered economic recovery. Instead, the economy plummeted and unemployment rates rose to afflict one in four American workers. This downward spiral set the stage for Hoover's defeat in 1932 by Democrat Franklin D. Roosevelt, who promised a New Deal.

After Roosevelt assumed the Presidency in 1933, Hoover became a spokesman in opposition to the domestic and foreign policies of the New Deal. Hoover's reputation dropped from being the most popular man for feeding millions to the most-ridiculed for being the cause of the Great Depression, of course, it wasn't true.

In 1947, President Harry S. Truman appointed Hoover to head the Hoover Commission, intended to foster greater efficiency throughout the federal bureaucracy. Most historians agree that Hoover's defeat in the 1932 election was caused primarily by the downward economic spiral, although his strong support for prohibition was also a significant factor.

Hoover is usually ranked lower than average among U.S.

Presidents.

45 THEY LED US INTO AND OUT OF THE GREAT DEPRESSION

The Great Depression that plagued the entire third decade of the 20th century took nearly as many years to create. Stock market speculation frenzy during the "Roaring" 1920s caused vast numbers of Americans to borrow money to buy stocks in the hope they would get rich quick. As their stock values grew, investors used held shares as collateral to buy yet even more, investing primarily in American industry.

By 1928, stockbrokers had loaned American investors millions. As stock values escalated through that year and into the next, a buying frenzy ensued. By September 1929, investors borrowed more than $800 million.

Unlike today's stock market, which has stringent federal and exchange safeguards brought about by the wild speculation of this earlier era, the boom of the '20s was unsteady primarily due to the tremendous amount of borrowed money and false optimism.

By October 1929, this tremendous debt caused the market to crash, and investors immediately lost confidence in their stocks. Loans were called resulting in a selling frenzy that caused a complete financial collapse. Those who sold their shares lost everything. Ironically, the few investors who held onto their stocks eventually regained their losses, which serve as a lesson for today's investors: what goes up comes down, but, eventually, it will go up again.

History shows the U.S. government had been short-sighted in its banking, securities, and economic policies, which contributed greatly to the "Crash of '29." Government's "hands-off" attitude toward American business resulted in unchecked investing and borrowing. The result was an unstable economy, with uneven national wealth. An American middle class was barely discernible. By 1930, the United States truly was a "have" and "have-not" nation. This is a lesson that shouldn't be forgotten.

Most of the nation's wealth was in the hands of a few families who hoarded their cash, or invested, rather than buying American goods. The supply of products became greater than their demand. While some people profited from this strategy, most did not. Prices began to rise to the point most Americans could not afford to buy very much. Farmers and workers were among the worst hit, causing a spiraling downward economy.

The 1920s were dominated by a Republican Executive Branch and Congress. Republican President Warren G. Harding succeeded Democrat Woodrow Wilson in 1921. When Harding died suddenly in 1923, Vice President Calvin Coolidge assumed office and held it until 1929 when another Republican, Herbert Hoover, took office.

President Hoover would have but a few months of peace and prosperity before the financial bottom dropped and the nation plunged into economic depression. By 1933, other modern nations followed and the entire world was in economic shambles.

Herbert Hoover became a tragic figure in American history. By the time he was elected president in 1928, Herbert Hoover was the single most popular man in America, and possibly, the world. He had an unparalleled reputation for public service. Hoover was an engineer by profession who became a public administrator and great world-renowned humanitarian.

Born in West Branch, Iowa, Hoover was the son of a Quaker blacksmith. A graduate of Stanford University, he worked in China where he became the leading engineer for an American company. He and his wife, Lou, were caught up in the Boxer Rebellion of 1900, where the future American president was credited with saving the lives of a number of young Chinese children.

This would be but the first episode where Hoover would come to the rescue of humanity.

When the First World War broke out in August 1914, Hoover was in London where the U.S. Consul General asked him for help in getting stranded American tourists in Europe out of harm's way. Hoover formed a rescue committee assisting some 120,000 fellow citizens escape the dangers of war.

With the war raging, Hoover led a U.S. effort to set about the coordination of food distribution to the people of Belgium, which had been overrun by the German army.

When the United States entered the war in 1917, President Wilson appointed Hoover to head up the U.S. Food Administration. Hoover succeeded in cutting domestic food consumption that would be needed for Europe, thus avoided rationing in the United States. Because of Hoover's efforts, no one in America or the Allied nations went hungry.

At war's end, Hoover was named to the Supreme Economic Council as well as head of the U.S. Relief Administration. This organization arranged food shipments to Germany and other war-torn central European nations. By 1921, Hoover extended U.S. aid to the Soviet Union, which was suffering a nationwide famine.

When Hoover was criticized for helping Communist Russia, he replied firmly: "There are 20 million people starving over there. Whatever their politics, they shall be fed!"

During the Harding and Coolidge administrations, Hoover served as U.S. Secretary of Commerce, positioning him to assume the GOP presidential nomination in 1928.

By March 1929, Americans couldn't have been more confident about their new president than with Herbert Hoover as he moved into the White House. America was booming with a vibrant stock market and a strong, bustling industry -- what could go wrong?

When the stock market crashed in October 1929, Hoover declared that a balanced budget and a tax cut, coupled with a spending expansion on public works would right the situation.

By 1931, similar economic woes in Europe were plunging the entire world into crisis and chaos. President Hoover presented a program for aiding American businesses and farmers, many of whom were facing foreclosures on their properties. He also proposed banking reforms; as well as, federal loans to states so they could feed their unemployed. Hoover also demanded the Federal government drastically cut its own spending wherever possible.

What has been lost to history is that Herbert Hoover was a kindly man who did have the best interests of the people at heart. However, while he felt no one should go hungry, Hoover maintained that the primary responsibility for feeding poor people was that of the individual states, local governments, and private volunteer organizations – not the Federal government. This would be a philosophy that would be his political ruin.

During his four years as president, Hoover had his detractors even in a Republican-controlled Congress. He accused politicians on both sides of the aisle of sabotaging his programs for their own political gain. As a result, Hoover was unfairly painted as a "callous and cruel president."

In 1932, Hoover was soundly defeated by former New York Gov. Franklin Delano Roosevelt, and was destined to be relegated to obscurity, but, that wasn't to be the case.

Years later, in 1947, President Harry Truman would appoint Hoover to help reorganize the executive departments of the government. When Truman was criticized by his fellow

Democrats for appointing "the man who caused the Great Depression," he simply replied, "Herbert Hoover didn't create the Depression, it was created for him."

There would be still more service to country by the kindly Quaker from Iowa. In 1953, President Dwight D. Eisenhower appointed Hoover as chairman of yet another governmental reorganization commission.

In all of his undertakings, with the exception of his four years as president, Hoover earned the admiration of his fellow citizens.

Hoover died at the age of 90 on Oct. 20, 1964, having served the U.S. government and its citizens longer and in more far-reaching ways than any other politician and humanitarian in American history. Yet, thanks to some short-sighted historians, today when his name is mentioned, people think of Herbert Hoover as the man who caused The Great Depression.

Unless one lived through the Depression, there's no way to fully explain what life in America was like for the average citizen. Jobs dried up causing money to be scarce. With the exception of those living in the "dust bowl" states of Oklahoma, northern Texas, and Kansas, people living in the vast rural areas of America often had plenty to eat because they were able to grow most of what was needed. But few had any hard currency to buy other necessities.

When work was available in the farming areas, earning a $1 a day was considered a good day's wages. In cities, life was even more cruel. It took money for everything, especially food. Thousands would line up for handouts, usually soup. Jobs were non-existent. Starvation and homelessness were commonplace.

By Election Day 1932, the American people were desperate for someone new to convince them he had a solution that would lead them back to the path of recovery. That man was Democrat Franklin Roosevelt.

FDR, as he became known to Americans, promoted his "New Deal." Roosevelt's plan quickly won the overwhelming support of the public.

President Roosevelt had something Hoover and most of the previous presidents, save FDR's cousin, Theodore Roosevelt, lacked: the backing of an entire nation. Within the first 100 days in office, FDR pushed dozens of programs through Congress to create jobs, provide relief, and get the economy jump-started. He had little resistance from politicians on both sides of the aisle, who were eager to report good news back in their home districts.

Ironically, most of Roosevelt's "New Deal" programs were based upon federal economic programs designed and started by Hoover during the First World War.

Unlike Hoover, FDR experimented, tossing things that didn't work and implementing programs that did. Roosevelt had something most presidents before, or after, never had: a unique ability to relate to the common, ordinary citizen. Despite being a wealthy man himself, FDR realized the American working man and woman were looking for change and he provided it for them.

As the Great Depression dragged through the 1930s, America struggled. Historians continue to argue whether FDR's economic programs would have ended the Depression. Today, however, history does reveal that President Roosevelt played a dangerous game during the late '30s and early '40s.

While most of the nation wanted nothing to do with the war in Europe, Great Britain was desperate for help. Roosevelt managed to provide arms and materials, even naval escorts for merchant ship convoys crossing the Atlantic, where scores of Nazi German submarine "wolf packs" patiently waited.

While Germany was over-running France, Hitler cast his eyes upon England. In May 1940, it was obvious to the Allied Forces that Hitler would be looking next at conquering England. Some two months before the Battle of Britain would begin, Roosevelt told an aide in the Oval Office on July 10, 1940, that something must be done "to help our English cousins" while continuing to maintain an neutral posture.

"We must find a way to help our friends, although I am a bit concerned about the fact that we're caught in the middle trying to stop empire builders in Asia (Japan), and Europe, (Germany and Italy) so that our English cousins might continue building their empire," Roosevelt lamented.

FDR and British Prime Minister, Winston S. Churchill, had met or exchanged letters on a number of occasions to make plans for war even though the U.S. was supposed to have been "neutral." There is evidence this collaboration had gone on even before Germany attacked Poland on Sept. 1, 1939, igniting World War II.

The President knew it would be a matter of time before the United States would be pulled into the war, and there was no doubt that America would be on the side of the Allied Forces. While the public focused upon the war news from Europe on the other side of the globe, the various invasions by Japan in Korea, Manchuria, China, and Southeast Asia were mostly ignored by Americans. After all, the Pacific was a big ocean and that conflict was a very long way from American shores.

The script nearly was completed when in 1940, Japan joined Germany and Italy to form the Axis powers. Roosevelt knew American forces would have to take action as Japanese forces came closer to U.S. installations in the Philippines, Guam, Midway, and Wake Island.

During those years leading up to the United States' entrance into the war, resource-stricken Japan had been buying great quantities of scrap metal, which was melted down and turned into implements of war. Much of it was flung back against the country from which it came.

The crowning blow in the Pacific, however, came when FDR placed an oil embargo against Japan, cutting off their critical petroleum supply. This forced Japan to become even more aggressive in Indonesia and Asia.

Much of Roosevelt's communications with Churchill were confidential and behind the scenes, while his public persona was that of an isolationist president. However, FDR never hid his contempt for Nazi Germany.

While Roosevelt secretly helped Churchill with Britain's defense plans, the President continued to tell Americans that he would do everything to keep the United States out of war, knowing full-well that only a miracle could prevent that from happening.

Roosevelt's full intentions finally were revealed in September 1940 when he proposed the "Lend-Lease" plan for Great Britain and the Soviet Union. The proposal was an answer to FDR's call for the loan of money, as well as, war materials such as ammunition, rifles, and other equipment to England and Russia.

Some 50 year-old World War I-era destroyers were turned over to British Royal Naval crews, while dozens of P-39 fighter aircraft and Studebaker trucks were shipped to the Soviet Union via merchant convoy. In return, the United States got 99-year leases for military bases in Newfoundland, Bermuda, and British Guiana.

To communicate directly with America, Roosevelt did something no other president had done -- he went on the radio to talk directly to the people. Previous presidents had issued press releases, and let the newspapers deliver the message; which often times, got distorted, turned around, or incorrectly presented. Much to the chagrin of America's press barons like Henry Luce, William Randolph Hearst, and Joseph Pulitzer, Roosevelt's nationwide radio "Fireside Chats" circumvented the media. His evening broadcasts on national radio were delivered when the entire family could gather around the radio. FDR came into every American home like an old friend, which made him one of the most charismatic presidents in U.S. history.

In his 1940 Lend-Lease speech to Congress and the American people, Roosevelt used the radio: "My fellow Americans ... England stands alone. ... We cannot, and we will not, tell them they have to surrender simply because we will not give them the weapons they need.

"If Great Britain goes down, then all of us in the Americas will be living at the point of a Nazi gun. ... I understand what

England's needs are, and I understand what the dangers are to both of us."

Later, Roosevelt told key members of his cabinet about his plans to assist Prime Minister Churchill far beyond Lend-Lease.

"Mr. Churchill and I will enter into a secret pact. For our part, we'll wage war against Nazi Germany, but not declare it. Everything must be done to create an incident."

Roosevelt pondered for a moment, and then admitted what those close to him already knew.

"You know, I'm a juggler. I never let my right hand know what my left hand does. I'm perfectly willing to mislead if it will help win the war. However, it's not that I mind walking a tightrope, but just how un-neutral can we get?"

By 1939, the economic effects of the Depression were beginning to lift. Because of the belligerent actions of Nazi Germany, and Italy in Europe, and the Japanese in Southeast Asia, the United States began to arm for war.

If there was one single man most responsible for the Allies winning the war against Fascism, it had to be Hungarian-born physicist Leo Szilard. Szilard (pronounced "So-lard"), along with fellow countryman Eugene Vigner. The two physicists had fled the Nazis in Europe, immigrating to the United States. Before he left, Szilard figured out a nuclear chain reaction was not only possible, but an atomic weapon could be made from it.

"If I've figured it out, then my colleagues back in Germany can do the same thing," he told noted physicist Albert Einstein in 1939. Szilard feared Hitler's scientists would develop an atomic weapon first.

"If that happens, the world will be lost to Hitler," Szilard maintained.

Szilard wanted President Roosevelt to know about the chain reaction possibility, but thought he wouldn't be taken seriously.

Einstein kept asking Szilard if such a reaction would be possible.

"How do you know this?" Einstein finally asked.

"I used your formula (E = MC 2) to figure it out!" Szilard exclaimed to an astonished Einstein.

Szilard pleaded with Einstein for two months, finally convincing him to sign a letter (written by Szilard) to the President.

The letter was dated July 16, 1939, and signed by Einstein. The letter to FDR informed him that nuclear chain reactions could be created and used in bombs. The letter was personally delivered by Alexander Sachs, a New York economist, who had been a speech writer for Roosevelt. It took three months for Sachs to get an appointment. Finally, on Oct. 11, 1939, Sachs was in the Oval office reading the letter to the President.

Knowing how important the letter was before he read it, Sachs got FDR's attention by telling him a story about Napoleon Bonaparte.

Sachs told the story of a young inventor-visionary who told the French Emperor he could build vessels that could travel the Channel to England at three-times the speed of present-day sailing ships.

As the story was told, Napoleon dismissed the young man as "a dreamer." The inventor was Robert Fulton, who built the first steam-powered ship.

With the story's point in mind, Sachs proceeded to inform Roosevelt of the powerful new weapon's possibilities.

Roosevelt gathered Szilard and other scientists with the nation's top military experts. It took nearly a year to convince the military of the potential, but when British agents informed American military leaders that Germany's main reason for invading Norway was to capture that nation's supply of "heavy water" to develop nuclear weapons, Szilard finally had the attention of officials in Washington.

As we now know, Roosevelt ordered the "Manhattan Project," which ultimately developed the atom bomb that ended the war in 1945. Ironically, FDR signed the directive authorizing the

Manhattan Project and the development of the atom bomb on December 6, 1941, the day before the Japanese attacked Pearl Harbor.

The build-up toward the Second World War had one redeeming quality: it put Americans back to work and money in their pockets -- something many had not had for a number of years. The build-up effectively ended the Great Depression.

By 1939, the American public was well on its way to economic recovery. The average income was $1,729; cost of a new house was $3,850; the average rent was $28 a month; a new car was $700; tuition to Harvard University was $420 yearly; gasoline was 10 cent a gallon; the average adult paid 25 cents to go to the movies; and a U.S. postage stamp was 3 cents.

The beginning of the end to the great World War II can be traced to a day in March of 1941 when President Roosevelt told the American people during one of his "Fireside Chat" radio broadcasts that "America must become the great arsenal of democracy. Let no man say it can't be done ... it must be done!" he demanded.

After years of military buildup and territorial intimidation, on Sept. 1, 1939, Nazi Germany unleashed its "Blitzkrieg" attack on a nearly defenseless Poland.

This unprovoked action brought Britain and France into the conflict to the defense of Poland. Within two years, nearly every modern nation around the globe had joined in, primarily with the Allies against the fascist states of Germany, Italy, and Japan.

After the Japanese attack on Pearl Harbor on Dec. 7, 1941, the American war machine cranked to full speed with nearly every able-bodied man and women becoming involved in one way or another. By 1942's end, factories across America were retooled from building sewing machines and automobiles to turning out more than 60,000 war planes, and countless tanks and guns. By 1943, the number of aircraft rose to 125,000.

Because President Roosevelt had the foresight to come to Great

Britain's aid in that nation's time of need, knowing that if England fell, America would stand alone in a hostile world. Instead, the United States led the Allies to victory.

Ironically, FDR would not live to see the end of the hostilities. He died on April 12, 1945, less than one month before Germany's surrender on May 8, and five months before his Manhattan Project delivered the world's first two atomic bombs, bringing Japan to unconditional surrender on Aug. 14, 1945.

While Szilard and Einstein were key to guiding the United States toward developing the ultimate weapon that ended the war, both regretted their actions. Einstein continued to work as a pacifist for the rest of his life, and Szilard refused to work any longer as a physicist and switched to biology. Still, without their vision and intellect, this book might have been written in a different language.

46 WHY HITLER SNUBBED THE AMERICAN BUND

During the 1930s, when the American economy was in shambles, many people were looking for a political savior – a different system of government that would take them out of the financial deep abyss. Some looked to socialism, others to communism. More than 30 percent of the nation was out of work, while the people of Germany were emerging from the Great Depression.

In 1936, a number of Americans having little faith in President Franklin D. Roosevelt and the U.S. government, joined, the German-American Bund, also known as the German-American Federation. It was a Nazi-leaning organization established in 1936. The Bund replaced a group known earlier as the Friends of New Germany. The new name emphasized the Bund's American foundation after public criticism that the Friends party was "unpatriotic." The Bund consisted primarily of German-American citizens.

The Bund's main goal was to promote a favorable view of Nazi Germany. The earlier "Friends" had been authorized in 1933, when Nazi Deputy Fuhrer Rudolf Hess gave German immigrant and Nazi party member, Heinz Spanknobel, the authority to form an American Nazi organization. Based in New York City, there was a strong "Friends" membership in Chicago and Milwaukee, both cities with large German-American populations. Spanknobel was deposed as leader when he was deported for failure to register as a foreign agent.

Like the earlier "Friends" organization, members of the new German-American Bund wore black uniforms, marched in parades, held weekend outings for families and gave the impression of a patriotic, family-oriented, all-American organization, all the while advocating a U.S. government in the image of Nazi Germany. A series of 69 Bund chapters were formed in the East and Midwest. Bund camps were set up as Nazi indoctrination and training facilities.

Using the swastika and Hitler salute, most of the Bund propaganda railed against President Roosevelt, the Jewish population, and Communists, but the Bund always professed loyalty to the United States by always displaying the American flag.

The Bund elected Fritz Kuhn, who had been a German soldier during World War I. He was granted U.S. citizenship in 1934. After assuming Bund control in March 1936, Kuhn was an effective leader. He was able to unite and expand the organization, but he was soon revealed to be an incompetent swindler, who had a tendency to exaggerate the truth.

Kuhn and a few of his "Bundsmen" traveled to Berlin for the 1936 Summer Olympics. They were ushered into the Reich Chancellery, where Kuhn had his photo taken with Adolf Hitler, who was not impressed. Hitler distrusted Kuhn and the Bund leadership, so the organization never received support from the Nazi regime.

The beginning of the end came when the Nazi government declared that no Nazi emblems were to be used by the Bund because Hitler needed to appease the U.S. government in distancing Germany from the organization, which had become a national embarrassment.

The Bund's activities peaked on Feb. 20, 1939, at a rally at Madison Square Garden in New York. More than 20,000 attended, where Kuhn criticized President Roosevelt, referring to his "Rosenfeld's New Jew Deal."

Later that year, Kuhn was charged with tax evasion and embezzling $14,000 from the Bund and was sentenced to prison.

When Hitler declared war on the United States in late 1941, it brought an end to the German-American Bund, which has become a mere footnote in history.

47 THE SPY WHO PLAYED PRO BASEBALL

There once was a most talented man, who was a Major League Baseball player, but his primary job was being a spy for the U.S. Government. He was Catcher Moe Berg.

In 1934, Berg was on the roster along with baseball legends Babe Ruth and Lou Gehrig when they went on a tour of Japan. Why would a bench-warming catcher be included among a team of all-stars?

He had two loves: baseball and spying. Because of this, Berg had been enlisted by the government because he spoke 15 different languages, including Japanese. The War Department (now known as the Department of Defense), was aware the Japanese were building a powerful Navy and information was needed.

While in Tokyo, Berg dressed in a kimono and took flowers to the daughter of an American diplomat, who was in the hospital --the tallest building in the Japanese capital, but he never delivered the flowers.

Berg climbed to the hospital's roof and with his movie camera filmed Tokyo Bay's, several military installations, factories, and rail yards. Eight years later, Lt. Col. Jimmy Doolittle used Berg's movies in planning the Tokyo raid.

While in high school Berg learned Latin, Greek, and French. He graduated Magna Cum Laude from Princeton where he learned Spanish, Italian, German, and Sanskrit. He did further studies at Paris' Sorbonne and Columbia Law School picking up Japanese, Chinese, Korean, Indian, Arabic, Portuguese, and Hungarian.

When the War Department found out about the amazing linguist, he quickly was recruited as a spy.

During World War II, Berg was in the OSS (Office of Strategic Services, a forerunner of the CIA).

He parachuted into Yugoslavia to assess the value of the two-partisan groups. He reported back that Marshall Tito's forces were widely supported by the people.

The question of the Nazis' progress building an Atomic bomb was Berg's next assignment. Under the code name "Remus," Berg was sent to Switzerland for a lecture by noted German physicist Werner Heisenberg.

Berg managed to slip past SS guards at the auditorium posing as a Swiss graduate student. Berg carried a pistol and a cyanide pill. If the scientist was to indicate the Nazis were close to building an atomic weapon, Berg was ordered to shoot him, and then swallow the cyanide pill. Sitting in the front row, Berg determined the Germans were nowhere near their goal, so he complimented Heisenberg on his speech and walked with the scientist back to his hotel.

In spite of being 41, Berg was to make more parachute jumps. He landed in German-held Norway where he met with underground fighters and located a secret heavy-water plant—part of the Nazis' effort to build an atomic weapon. His intel guided the Royal Air Force in a bombing raid to destroy the plant.

Berg's report from Norway had been distributed to Britain's Prime Minister, Winston Churchill, President Franklin D. Roosevelt and key figures in the team in Los Alamos, who were developing the atomic bomb. President Roosevelt remarked: "Give my regards to the catcher."

After the war, Berg was awarded the Medal of Merit by President Harry Truman. The honor was America's highest civilian war time recognition. Berg declined the honor because he couldn't reveal his spying activities.

Berg played for six Major League teams, the last being the Boston Red Sox (1935-39).

After his death in 1972, Berg's sister accepted his Medal of Merit and today it's displayed in the Baseball Hall of Fame in Cooperstown, New York.

48 'THE BATTLING BASTARDS OF BATAAN'

One of the best examples of America at its most unprepared and inept was the retreat of the untrained, ill-equipped with obsolete weapons, and poorly led U.S. Army units on the main Philippine island of Luzon. The 75,000-plus army of both American and Filipino soldiers battled in futility against the Japanese onslaught.

From Dec. 8, 1941 to April 9, 1942, the American and Filipino soldiers fought fiercely and bravely, but ended up being trapped and forced to surrender. As the Japanese advanced, hundreds of Filipino soldiers began tossing their weapons and blowing up ammunition dumps as they retreated southward on the Bataan peninsula, trying to escape.

In the meantime, the Japanese air and naval forces pounded the fortress island of Corregidor at the mouth of Manila Bay where General Douglas McArthur, commander of all Philippine forces, had retreated from Manila.

The escape of McArthur from Corregidor was nothing short of a miracle. The U.S. Navy whisked McArthur and his family from Corregidor, weaving through the various islands, dodging Japanese warships and eventually south to Australia.

While much has been written about McArthur's valiant escape, less has been documented about what he left behind: An army in disarray, disillusioned, and demoralized. In the eyes of many soldiers who were there, McArthur abandoned his command, even though he acted on the order of President Franklin D. Roosevelt.

Despite McArthur's explanation that he "reluctantly" left the Philippines, the general quickly became known among the troops as "Dugout Doug." As unfair as that moniker might have been, to those who survived the march of death to prison camps that was to come, had quite another opinion.

McArthur overestimated the ability of his command, and underestimated the Japanese. When defenders failed to turn back the Japanese on the eastern beaches of Luzon, McArthur retreated his troops across Manila Bay to Bataan, leaving most of their ammunition and food supplies on the beaches that had been overrun by the enemy.

One little-known fact: of the 75,000 man army, three-quarters were Filipinos, with the remainder American. Other than the highly-skilled Philippine Scouts, most of the troops, both U.S. and Filipino, were poorly trained and ill-equipped for meeting the battle-hardened Japanese army. To give some idea of the disorganization, the main body of Filipino soldiers spoke the Bicolanian dialect, whereas most of the officers spoke only Tagalog; American soldiers spoke neither.

Regardless of the disarray of the American and Filipino forces, a tremendous four-month battle was fought with Filipino and American troops inflicting heavy Japanese losses.

Toward the end, lack of food became critical. Food rations were cut in half. Of the 250 horses and 48 pack mules, most ended up being what became known as "cavalry steak."

By March 1942, the only U.S. war correspondent left in the Philippines, summed the situation up in a poem, which was sent back to the American public:

"We're the battling bastards of Bataan,
No mama, no pap, no Uncle Sam,

No aunts, no uncles, no cousins, no nieces,
No pills, no planes, no artillery pieces,
And nobody gives a damn."

On April 9, Lt. Gen. Jonathan Wainwright reluctantly surrendered his beleaguered troops to the Japanese. It was the end of the fighting, but the beginning of the torturous march to the POW camps. It became known as a "March of Death."

As one general wrote years later about the Battle of Bataan … "In full truth, it was an unsavory mess.".

49 THE BATAAN DEATH MARCH

It was arguably the largest and longest forced-march of humans in known history. The transfer of American and Filipino prisoners 80 miles up the Bataan peninsula beginning April 9, 1942, ending a month later, took an undetermined death toll. Exact numbers may never be known due to the many prisoners who drifted off, blending into the civilian population as they marched along the road from Mariveles near Corregidor.

After marching some 80 miles north to San Fernando, the prisoners were then crammed into unventilated box cars and taken by rail to Capas, where they then were forced to walk the final nine miles to Camp O'Donnell. Some 100 or more prisoners were stuffed into each of the rail cars. The rail cars had no sanitation facilities and even more of the POWs died.

Environmental surroundings caused more deaths than the soldiers. All along the march, thousands of prisoners died from fatigue in the sweltering tropical heat, which caused even more deaths and sickness.

The death toll "estimate" is between 2,500 to 10,000 Filipinos, along with 100 to 650 American prisoners. The high fatality rates of both military and civilians inflicted by the Japanese army was deemed a "war crime" by an Allied military commission after the War.

The Japanese army was totally unprepared to handle as many as 80,000 prisoners. The brutality inflicted upon the American and Filipino prisoners was unimaginable. Trucks following the march, ran over prisoners who fell in the road. Those who collapsed from fatigue, hunger, and thirst, too weak to continue, were shot or bayoneted by Japanese soldiers in what was known as the "clean-up crew."

Even those who managed to stay on their feet and continue walking were harassed with random bayonet stabs and beatings. The Japanese soldiers considered their prisoners to be "sub-human" because the prisoners had committed the unspeakable act of surrendering instead of dying in combat, which was a Japanese belief.

Even after reaching Camp O'Donnell, prisoners continued to die at the rate of 30 to 50 per day. Most of the dead were buried in mass graves the Japanese had dug with bulldozers outside the barbed-wire compound.

The Bataan Death March was not known to the American public until January 1944, when sworn statements were released by the government of U.S. Army officers who had escaped.

General of the Army, George Marshall, said at the public disclosure, "… We serve notice upon the Japanese military and political leaders, as well as, the Japanese people that the future of the Japanese race itself, depends entirely and irrevocably upon their capacity to progress beyond their aboriginal barbaric instincts."

After the Japanese surrender, General Masaharu Homma was held responsible for the Bataan Death March. A war crimes tribunal found him guilty. He was executed outside of Manila on April 3, 1946.

It wasn't until May 9, 2009, that the Japanese government formally apologized through its ambassador to the U.S. to all former American prisoners of war who suffered in the Bataan Death March. Unfortunately, the apology came too late for most of the survivors. By 2009, most survivors had died of old age or disease -- many of which were maladies the result of their Bataan ordeal.

50 THE COOK WHO WAS AN UNLIKELY HERO

The under-fire actions of a low-ranking Navy cook during the attack on Pearl Harbor, made the sailor one of the first Americans decorated for bravery during World War II.

What adds interest to the actions of "Dorey" Miller, a third-class petty officer, was that he was the first African-American to be so recognized. As a result, his heroism rallied the Black communities across America to give more support the war effort.

Miller was a cook aboard the USS West Virginia. When the attack on Pearl Harbor began, he immediately reported to his battle station, only to discover a torpedo had destroyed it.

The young petty officer ran into an officer, who told him to go to the bridge and aid the ship's Captain Mervyn Bennion, who had been hit by shrapnel.

Miller was then ordered to load two Browning .50 caliber anti-aircraft machine guns in the aft part of the battleship. He wasn't familiar with the machine gun, but two accompanying officers told him what to do.

Miller fired the gun until he ran out of ammunition, then he was ordered to help carry the Captain up to the navigation bridge out of the thick oily smoke generated by the many fires on and around the ship.

When the attack finally subsided, Miller was ordered to help move injured sailors through oil and water, thereby "unquestionably saving the lives of a number of people who might otherwise have been lost."

The West Virginia sank to the harbor bottom as her crew—including Miller—abandoned ship.

Two weeks later, the Navy released a list of commendations. Among them was a single notation for an "unnamed Negro." The NAACP asked President Franklin D. Roosevelt to determine the name of the sailor and award him the Distinguished Service Cross, at that time the second-highest combat honor. The Navy Board of Awards in Washington D. C., revealed the name of the "unknown Negro" sailor was Third Class Petty Officer "Doris Miller." The Pittsburgh Courier initiated a write-in campaign to send Miller to the Naval Academy.

His combat recognition made him one of the first heroes of World War II. He was commended by Secretary of the Navy Frank Knox, and personally recognized by Fleet Admiral Chester W. Nimitz aboard the aircraft carrier USS Enterprise. Nimitz presented Miller with the Navy Cross, the third-highest award for gallantry during combat the Navy awarded at the time. Today, the Navy Cross is the second-highest honor for the Navy and Marines.

Miller was promoted to Mess Attendant First Class on June 1, 1942. The Pittsburgh Courier continued to push to return Miller to the U.S. for a war bond tour, but he already was back in the country doing just that.

After training in Hawaii, Miller was assigned to the USS Liscome Bay, which took part in the Battle of Makin Island. On November 24, that ship was sunk with only 272 survivors from the crew of more than 900. Miller was not among them.

Dorey Miller has slipped into historical obscurity; however, actor Cuba Gooding played Miller in a few brief scenes in the recent film, "Pearl Harbor," which returned the sailor's heroism.

51 AN UNBELIEVABLE EFFORT OF PRODUCTION

Between 1940 and 1946, the United States became the most powerful nation in the world. This came about because of World War II.

Anyone who wanted a job got one – unemployment was a forgotten memory of the Great Depression.

The nation rose from being a sleeping giant to an industrial juggernaut that built not only the largest armed force in history, with an arsenal of war materials that not only equipped our nation's military, but that of a number of other Allied nations such as Great Britain, France, Canada, China, the Soviet Union, and others.

Because of the war, America's Great Depression was ended due to the great demand of war products, which put the nation back to work. During the period from 1940 through 1945, the United States produced more material from implements of war to uniforms and food stuffs than had been produced by all nations in a century of time before the War.

To give an approximate picture of the enormity of America's wartime production, consider the following data taken from several historical accounts:

For the Navy, there were 22 aircraft carriers built, as well as 8 battleships, 48 cruisers, 349 destroyers, 420 destroyer escorts, 203 submarines, and 34 million tons of merchant ships, also known as "Liberty Ships."

Shipbuilding companies were turning out troop-carrying and supply vessels in record numbers. Kaiser Shipbuilding in Oakland was able to increase its production by launching a "Liberty Ship" every 30 days.

Aviation-wise there were 100,000 fighter aircraft built, as well as, 98,000 bombers, 24,000 transport planes, and 58,000 training aircraft. Several automobile companies switched their production lines to building bombers and other large aircraft.

Ford and General Motors turned out B-24 "Liberators" by the hundreds. Consolidated Aircraft Co., in San Diego. assembled bombers in huge factories shielded by a mammoth camouflaged canopy that, from above, made it look like a pastoral landscape of farms and fields.

Boeing was turning out huge numbers of B-17s and other aircraft at its plants in Seattle and Moses Lake in the state of Washington, as well as, Wichita, Kansas.

Goodyear Rubber was turning out all sorts of tires and other war materials, including rubber, self-sealing fuel bladder wing tanks for B-29s in Lincoln, Nebraska, and Akron, Ohio.

For the Army and Marine Corps, 93,000 tanks were built along with 257,000 artillery pieces, 105,000 mortars, 3 million machine guns, and 2.5 million military trucks. A variety of farm implement manufacturers and sewing machine companies turned to making small arms such as pistols and rifles.

The Studebaker automobile company built trucks, thousands of them sent to Russia on the Lend-Lease plan. Soviet veterans maintained years after the war that the most valuable equipment they had to fight with was the Studebaker truck because of its reliability in the rugged Russian terrain.

Willys-Overland, American Bantam Car Co., and Ford Motor Co., responded to a U.S. War Department request to design a utility vehicle which became known as the "Jeep." The name, "Jeep" is slang for "General Purpose" vehicle, which was at first referred to simply as a "GP," then it was gradually slurred into "Jeep" by adoring GIs.

Hundreds of small manufacturing companies produced millions of rounds of ammunition of a variety of calibers, as well as, thousands of hand grenades, bombs, and other high explosives. Clothing manufacturers made all types of uniforms, gear, and combat-wear.

Food companies produced millions of tons of food stuffs to feed the armed forces while the civilian population went to rationing food and many other items from clothing to gasoline to rubber tires.

There were 16.1 million men and women in uniform throughout the various armed services, and double that amount of civilians working in all of the war production factories around the clock, seven-days-a week.

Almost overnight, beginning in 1940, America went from a sleepy, isolationist nation to that of the most powerful in the world.

American forces invaded Africa, Sicily, and Italy, won the battle for the Atlantic, planned and executed D-Day, marched across the Pacific and Europe, developed the atomic bomb, and ultimately conquered Japan and Germany. Nothing in the history of mankind has ever equaled the multilayers of production toward a singular purpose: that of winning a world war.

52 THE "WILD" FATHER OF U.S. INTELLIGENCE

While the United States had spies as far back as the Revolutionary War, things didn't get tightly organized until just before World War II.

Army Col. William J. "Wild Bill" Donovan organized the Office of Strategic Services (OSS), forerunner of the Central Intelligence Agency (CIA). He is recognized as the "Father of American Intelligence services."

Born in 1883, Donovan held a number of positions as soldier, lawyer, diplomat, but most famously, he was an intelligence officer. A decorated veteran of World War I, Donovan is the only person to have received all four of the United States' highest awards: The Medal of Honor, the Distinguished Service Cross, the Distinguished Service Medal, and the National Security Medal.

Donovan was a football star at Columbia University where he was known as "Wild Bill." Before World War II, Donovan traveled extensively in Europe, and met with foreign leaders including Benito Mussolini of Italy. Donovan's belief a second major war was inevitable earned him the attention of **President Franklin D. Roosevelt**.

Germany's invasion of Poland in September 1939, was an action Donovan had predicted. Accordingly, Roosevelt gave him a number of increasingly important assignments as the U.S. prepared for war.

During 1940-41, Donovan traveled to England to assess Britain's ability to defend against Germany's aggression. Donovan met with **Winston Churchill** and the various directors of Britain's intelligence services. He returned to the U.S. confident of Britain's chances and developing plans for an American intelligence service modeled on the British Secret Services.

At the time, America's foreign intelligence organizations were fragmented and isolated from each other. The Army, Navy, Federal Bureau of Investigation, United States Department of State, and other interests each ran their own intelligence operations, the results of which was a reluctance to share information.

The Office of Strategic Services was established by Roosevelt on June 13, 1942, charged to collect and analyze strategic information required by the Joint Chiefs of Staff, and to conduct special operations. During the War, the OSS grew to nearly 24,000 people.

Donovan's OSS eventually conducted successful espionage and sabotage operations in Europe and parts of Asia.

At the end of the War, Donovan focused on preserving the OSS. As a result of President Roosevelt's death, Donovan's political position, was substantially weakened.

Although he argued forcefully for the OSS's retention, Donovan was opposed by many, including **President Harry S. Truman**, who personally disliked Donovan, and **J. Edgar Hoover**, who saw Donovan as a threat to the FBI. Accordingly, Truman officially disbanded the OSS in September 1945, a month after Japan surrendered.

For many years the operations of the OSS remained secret, but by the 1970s and 1980s, significant parts of the OSS exploits were declassified resulting in it becoming fodder for books and movies.

Having led the OSS during wartime, Donovan's opinion was influential in forming a new service. He argued the new agency should be able to conduct covert action. Truman didn't like that aspect, but Donovan won the argument, and it was reflected in the Central Intelligence Agency Act of 1949.

Major General William "Wild Bill" Donovan, one of America's most-decorated soldiers and civil servants, will be most remembered not only for his wartime covert actions, but his contributions in developing America's present-day CIA. Donovan died Feb. 8, 1959, of dementia, sadly, unable to remember his fascinating life. He is buried in Arlington National Cemetery.

53 THE 'WORLD'S MOST BEAUTIFUL INVENTOR'

She was a popular Hollywood and international film star, who not only was one of the great beauties on screen, but became an important inventor that greatly aided the Allied effort during World War II.

Born Hedwig Eva Maria Kiesler to a Jewish family on November 9, 1914, the world would come to know her as: Hedy Lamarr.

Her early and brief film career in Germany included controversial nude and love-making scenes in the 1933 film "Ecstasy,"

In 1933, Lamarr married her first of six husbands, Max Mandl, a wealthy Austrian military arms merchant, who was very controlling. She often would accompany Mandl to business meetings where he conferred with scientists involved in military technology. These conferences became her introduction to the field of applied science that nurtured her latent talent in the scientific field. Mandl, himself half-Jewish, often entertained Adolf Hitler and Benito Mussolini at dinner parties, as well as, selling arms and munitions to them.

After escaping her tyrannical husband in 1937, Lamarr fled to Paris where she met MGM's Louis B. Mayer. The Hollywood mogul hired her, insisting she change her name to "Hedy Lamarr". Upon arriving in Hollywood in 1938, Mayer promoted her as the "world's most beautiful woman."

Lamarr made 18 films from 1940 to 1949. After leaving MGM in 1945, she enjoyed her biggest success as Delilah in Cecil B. DeMille's "Samson and Delilah," with Victor Mature -- the highest-grossing film of 1949.

At the beginning of the World War II, Lamarr helped the U.S. war effort by selling War Bonds, but also by using her scientific knowledge. Lamarr began developing the invention for which she would become famous.

Lamarr co-invented the technology for "Spread Spectrum" and "Frequency Hopping" communications with composer/pianist George Antheil. The new technology became important to America's military during the War because it was used in controlling torpedoes. Today, those inventions have been incorporated into the modern Wi-Fi, CDMA and Bluetooth technology.

The U.S. Navy used the early WWII version of frequency hopping in 1962 during the Cuban Missile Crisis.

Between films, Lamarr usually kept her technical mind busy by inventing to relieve her boredom. Among her earliest inventions were an improved traffic signal and a carbonated beverage. The beverage was not successful -- she claimed it tasted like Alka-Seltzer.

Her later years were not happy ones. In 1966, she was arrested for shoplifting in Los Angeles. The charges were eventually dropped. In 1991, she was arrested on the same charge in Florida, this time for $21.48 worth of laxatives and eye drops. Both charges were dropped upon her promise not to repeat the offenses.

In 1997, Lamarr and Antheil received recognition for their invention by the Electronic Frontier Foundation Pioneer Award and the Gnass Spirit of Achievement Bronze Award, which are given to individuals whose creative lifetime achievements in the arts, sciences, business, or invention fields have significantly contributed to society. Her technical contributions have been featured on the Science Channel and Discovery Channel.

In 2014, Lamarr and Antheil were inducted into the National Inventor's Hall of Fame.

For her movie contributions, Lamarr has a star on the Hollywood Walk of Fame.

At age 85, Lamarr died in Casselberry, Florida, on January 19, 2000. Her son, Anthony Loder, took her ashes to Austria and spread them in the Vienna Woods, in accordance with her last wishes. She was given an honorary grave in Vienna's Central Cemetery in 2014.

54 RATIONING DURING WORLD WAR II

For civilians during World War II, rationing was introduced in stages, which was a process that controlled the size and frequency of a number of items used in everyday life.

In the summer of 1941, the British government appealed to the United States to conserve food in order to provide a bigger supply to be shipped to Brits, who were already fighting the Germans. They were being starved out by constant bombings and U-boat attacks on shipping. The "Office of Price Administration" warned Americans of potential gasoline, steel, aluminum, and electricity shortages.

After the attack on Pearl Harbor, of most concern was a shortage of rubber since the Japanese controlled the rubber-producing regions of Southeast Asia. Throughout the war, rationing of gasoline was motivated by a desire to conserve rubber. Accordingly, tires were the first item to be rationed by the OPA, which ordered the temporary end of sales December 11, 1942.

"The War Production Board" (WPB) ordered the temporary end of all civilian automobile sales on Jan. 1, 1942, leaving dealers with a half million unsold cars. Only certain professions qualified to purchase the remaining new car inventory.

By early February of 1942, automobile factories ceased manufacturing civilian models and converted to producing ships, aircraft, tanks, trucks, cannons, and other military products with the United States government as the only customer.

May 4, 1942, civilians first received ration books through more than 100,000 schoolteachers, PTA groups, and other volunteers. A national speed limit of 35-miles per hour was imposed to save fuel and rubber for tires. Each person in a household received a ration book, including babies and small children, who qualified for canned milk not available to others.

To receive a gasoline ration card, a person had to certify a need and ownership of no more than five tires. All tires over five were confiscated.

Gas rationing was by category:

An "A" sticker on a car was the lowest priority of gasoline rationing and entitled the car owner to 3 to 4 gallons per week.

"B" stickers were issued to workers in the military industry, entitling their holder up to 8 gallons per week.

"C" stickers were granted to persons deemed very essential to the war effort, such as doctors.

"T" rations were made available for truckers.

Lastly, "X" stickers on cars entitled the holder to unlimited supplies and were the highest priority in the system, including ministers, police, firemen, and civil defense workers.

Anyone wishing to purchase a new metal tube of toothpaste had to turn in an empty one. Sugar was rationed a half-a-pound per person per week -- half of normal consumption. Bakeries and ice cream makers received rations of about 70 percent their normal usage.

Because of German U-boat attacks on shipping from Brazil, coffee was rationed one pound every five weeks, about half of normal consumption. Other rationing included gasoline, bicycles, footwear, silk, nylon, fuel oil, stoves, meat, lard, shortening and oils, cheese, butter, margarine, processed foods (canned, bottled, and frozen), dried fruits, canned milk, firewood and coal, jams, jellies, and fruit butter.

Penicillin was rationed by the military. Hospitals received only small amounts. Each hospital decided which patients would receive the wonder antibiotic.

There was a black market in ration stamps. The OPA ordered vendors not to accept stamps they themselves did not tear out of books.

As a result of the gasoline rationing, all forms of automobile racing and sightseeing were banned.

In 1946, a year after the War ended, all rationing ended.

55 AMERICA'S REAL HERO MOVIE STAR

During World War II, dozens of movie luminaries donned military uniforms, but none would equal the service-to-country of James Stewart. He became a B-24 bomber pilot flying more than 25 combat missions while gathering a handful of military honors, including two Distinguished Flying Crosses, the Air Force's highest honor.

James "Jimmy" Maitland Stewart, who was born May 20, 1908, became a popular film actor, known for his distinctive drawl voice and down-to-earth persona. He starred in dozens of films now considered classics. In films, Stewart portrayed the average American man with everyday struggles.

In October 1940, Stewart was drafted into the U.S. Army, but was rejected because he was under the minimum 148 pounds. Stewart then attempted to enlist in the Army Air Corps, but still couldn't meet the weight requirement. He persuaded the recruiting officer to tweak the weigh-in, resulting in success.

A college graduate and a licensed commercial pilot, Stewart applied for a pilot commission. At age 33, he was six years beyond the maximum age restriction for cadet training. But in 1942, shortly after the Pearl Harbor attack, Stewart became a 2nd lieutenant.

Even though Stewart did not want to be a celebrity trotted out to sell war bonds, his first assignment was a rally in Washington, D.C. He wanted a combat unit rather than be a recruiting symbol. But in early 1942, before his additional training, Stewart made a short recruiting nationwide film, "Winning Your Wings," resulting in 150,000 new recruits.

Stewart finally was assigned to a combat unit, but he was 35 years old and getting into combat seemed impossible. His 30-year-old commanding officer understood and recommended Stewart to a B-24 Liberator unit.

Stewart was assigned to the 445th Bomb Group as operations officer. The group flew its first combat mission on December 13, 1943, bombing the U-boat pens at Kiel, Germany.

Later, Stewart was promoted to Major and awarded the Distinguished Flying Cross for actions as deputy group commander.

Stewart received a second award of the Distinguished Flying Cross for actions in combat and was awarded France's Croix de Guerre. He also received the Air Medal.

Stewart was promoted to full colonel on March 29, 1945. He became commanding officer of the 2nd Bomb Wing. Stewart was one of the few Americans to rise from private to colonel in four years.

After the War, the iconic actor continued to play a role in the United States Air Force Reserve. Stewart received permanent promotion to colonel in 1953, and served as Air Force Reserve Commander of Dobbins Air Reserve Base. In 1959, Stewart was promoted to Brigadier General. During his active duty periods, he remained current as a pilot of the B-36, the B-47, and B-52 intercontinental bombers of the Strategic Air Command.

On Feb. 20, 1966, Brigadier General Stewart flew as an observer on a B-52 bombing mission during the Vietnam War. He refused any publicity on that flight because he didn't want it treated as a stunt, but as part of his job as an officer in the Reserve. In 1968, after 27 years of service, Stewart retired from the Air Force. Later he was promoted to Major General on the retired list by President Ronald Reagan.

During his long film career, he was nominated five times for an Oscar, winning "Best Actor" for "The Philadelphia Story," in 1940. James Stewart died on July 2, 1997, at the age of 89.

56 FIELD MARSHAL ROMMEL: THE DESERT FOX

During the 20th century, there were a number of renowned and highly-respected military leaders – Pershing, Eisenhower, Patton, Bradley, MacArthur, Marshall, Yamamoto, Montgomery, but none had the unique admiration of both friend and foe as that of Germany's Erwin Rommel.

Erwin Johannes Eugen Rommel, popularly known as "The Desert Fox," was a German field marshal during World War II. He was born on Nov. 15, 1891, in a part of the German Empire. He was commissioned a lieutenant in the German Army in January 1912.

Rommel met his wife, Lucie, and married on Nov. 27, 1916. Their only son, Manfred, would become Lord Mayor of Stuttgart from 1974 to 1996. He died on Nov. 7, 2013.

Rommel's reward for his 1940 "Ghost Division" successes in France was promotion to the rank of lieutenant general. He had a reputation as an elite commander of motorized forces and was appointed to lead the newly-created Deutsches Afrika Korps (DAK). He was sent to Libya to aid demoralized Italian troops. Because of his bold successes, British journalists dubbed him "The

Desert Fox."

Never a member of the Nazi Party, Rommel is regarded as having been a humane and professional officer. His Afrika Korps were never accused of war crimes, and soldiers captured during his Africa campaign were reported to have been treated with dignity. Hitler's orders to kill Jewish soldiers, civilians, and captured commandos were ignored.

Late in the war during Rommel's last command of the Atlantic Wall prior to D-Day, Hitler ordered him to deport the area's Jewish population -- Rommel disobeyed. He refused Hitler's order to execute Jewish POWs, and directed that French workers be paid for their labor, and not be used as slave laborers. An RCAF Spitfire strafed him while traveling in his staff convertible. Rommel was thrown from the car, suffering cuts to his face and three skull fractures.

Early in 1944, three of Rommel's closest friends began efforts to bring Rommel into an anti-Hitler "Valkerie" conspiracy. They felt he would lend their cause credibility with the people. Rommel agreed to the conspiracy in order to, as he put it, "...to come to the rescue of Germany."

After the failed July 20, 1944, bombing attempt, conspirators were arrested – including Rommel. On Oct. 14, 1944, the field marshal was visited by two generals from Hitler's headquarters. He was informed of the charges and was offered a choice: face the People's Court or quietly commit suicide. If suicide, he would be assured his family full pension and a state funeral claiming he had died a hero. Rommel took a cyanide capsule. The truth behind his death became known to the Allies when Rommel's widow was interviewed in April 1945. The public did not know the details until the Nuremberg Trials.

When Rommel's involvement in the attempt to kill the Nazi leader became known after the war, his stature was enhanced in the eyes of his former adversaries. Rommel became the most widely-known and well-regarded leader in the German Army. In 1970, a

German Navy destroyer was named "The Rommel" in his honor. For decades after the war on the anniversary of his death, veterans of the Africa campaign, including former opponents, would gather at Rommel's tomb in Herrlingen.

Writing about Rommel years after the war, Winston Churchill offered the following: "His ardour, and daring, inflicted grievous disasters upon us. ... He also deserves our respect ... (but) ... in the wars of modern democracy, there is little place for chivalry.

57 THE DEADLY SKIES OVER EUROPE

One haunting thought that would never leave the upper-most mind of any crewmember of an Allied plane flying over enemy territory was having to evade and escape in case they were shot down. Thousands of Allied fliers found themselves in such a predicament -- on the ground, scurrying for a hiding place. Some successfully made it back to friendly territory; many others were captured or, worse, killed.

The dilemma facing downed fliers was: *Do I stay in uniform and try to get back to safety? Or, do I get into civilian clothes and blend into the society while making good my escape?*

The answer was easy, but getting into civilian clothes took them out of the security of the Geneva Convention rules, and into the category of being a suspected spy. Here is the harrowing example of what happened to one downed flier who shed his uniform to mask his identity.

Thousands of Allied fliers were forced to bail out of their crippled aircraft, or crash-landed after being hit by enemy fire while flying on bombing missions over Europe. Those not immediately captured by the Germans attempted to get back to friendly territory by evading the enemy often with the help of friendly resistance fighters, primarily in France, Belgium, and Holland. When fliers would be caught wearing civilian clothes they could be treated like spies. Most were ultimately identified as Allied prisoners of war and placed in POW camps. A few, however, weren't so lucky. One of the most dramatic stories comes as a result of 162 known Allied fliers who ended up in Buchenwald Concentration Camp.

William H. "Bill" Ryherd of Oceanside spent three months in a hell on earth in late 1944, when he was held as a prisoner in Nazi Germany's infamous Buchenwald death camp.

Ryherd found himself inside of one of Hitler's concentration camps not because of religious or political beliefs, but because he was caught by the Gestapo in Paris while out of his U.S. Army Air Corps uniform trying to escape to Spain.

According to Geneva Convention rules, POW status isn't required if the uniform isn't worn. As far as the Germans were concerned, he was just another civilian working against the Third Reich.

Ryherd, a native of Donna, Texas, was a first lieutenant assigned to the U.S. 9th Air Force flying a B-26 out of England. He was shot down on his 36th mission on Aug. 4, 1944. Ryherd was supposed to have taken a 10-day leave in Scotland after his 35th mission with the 397th Bombing Group, in the 598th Bombing Squadron flying out of Rivenhall, England, but he wanted to be part of a new type of bombing called "A-zone."

A-zone was the first radio-directed bombs used in the war. The new device required the pilot fly a steady course while the bombardier guided the bombs to their target. It turned out to be a fatal move. The target was a bridge over the Seine River a few miles south of Paris. Two bursts of enemy flak ripped through Ryherd's wing tank, causing a fire. As long as fuel was leaking and the fire burning, Ryherd knew he was okay. It was when the tank was drained that vapors would explode. He had to act fast.

"I had my crew bail out," Ryherd recalled. "I tried to stay with it as long as I could, but soon after they were out, I got out of there myself."

Ryherd dropped out of his plane through the bomb bay doors at 12,000 feet using a chest parachute, which wouldn't open.

"I literally tore it (parachute) open with my hands," he recalled. "About that time my plane blew up. I got out just in time."

Ryherd landed in an open French farmer's field where workers were tilling the soil.

"I grabbed my 'chute and ran about 100 yards into the woods," he said. "I didn't know it at the time, but I had broken my ankle when I landed."

A French resistance fighter happened to be one of the workers in the field. Neither spoke the other's language, but the Frenchmen made himself understood by pointing to his watch. The farm worker would come back at midnight for the American airman.

"This guy scooped up my 'chute and took off," Ryherd chucked. "I didn't know whether he'd bring back help or the Germans."

About midnight, the Frenchman returned with a comrade. Both were armed with automatic weapons. Ryherd went to get up out of his hiding place, discovering for the first time he had a broken ankle.

The trio traveled into a small village where a college professor hid Ryherd during the next few days. As relieved as Ryherd was that he was in the hands of the French resistance, he became nervous when the man who found him explained that "about 30 percent of the resistance fighters were loyal to France; about 30 percent to the Germans; and another 40 percent would play both sides of the fence, depending upon circumstances.

After several days of rest, the French moved Ryherd to another house where he found his co-pilot. From there, the French resistance fighters said it was possible to escape back to Allied lines from Paris by going west through the Pyrenees Mountains and into Spain. They drove into the French capital, which was still in German control. By this time, the two Americans had changed into civilian clothing.

"When we arrived in Paris, we could hear (General George) Patton's big guns to the north of the city," Ryherd said.

The resistance placed the two Yanks at a house in Paris where there was another Allied flier, a downed RAF pilot. The plan was to disguise all three fliers as part of a work gang of Frenchmen. Once outside of the city, they'd make there way to the Pyrenees Mountains and cross over into Spain and freedom.

"On the day we were to leave, came a knock on the door -- one with the right code, only it came about an hour early," Ryherd recalled. "It was one of the Frenchmen resistance guys we'd met in Paris. We went downstairs and my co-pilot and the British flier were waiting in the car. We headed out of Paris in the right direction (south), but suddenly the driver swerved with a hard turn and we drove right in Gestapo headquarters."

Ryherd and his comrades were betrayed by a French resistance fighter called "Captain Jacque." This wouldn't be the first time Jacque would betray Allied fliers. After the war, he would be tried as a war criminal and hung. But, on this day in 1944, he would be responsible for sending Ryherd to hell on earth.

Ryherd couldn't believe the betrayal by the Frenchman, but he remembered the caution another Frenchman had given him a few days before. It was true.

"When we arrived at Gestapo Headquarters, there were German soldiers everywhere burning documents and scurrying around," Ryherd said. "They knew Patton was coming and they were trying to get out of our town."

Ryherd was surprised their interrogation was so quick and even somewhat sloppy. The airmen confessed to being Allied fliers, but the Gestapo interrogator pointed out they were in civilian clothes, no dog tags, so they must be civilians. The trio was taken to a prison where some 3,000 French men and women were being held.

It is ironic that Allied military politics prevented Ryherd and his comrades from being rescued by General Patton.

"Ike (General Dwight D. Eisenhower) made Patton halt outside of Paris until General (Charles) DeGaulle could get into position to lead the Allied troops into the city," Ryherd said. "This delay gave the Germans a chance to ship all of us in that prison out of town on railroad cars."

The next five days were a precursor to what lie ahead. Among the 2,000 men and 1,000 women jammed 95-plus into railroad cars designed to hold only 40 people, were some 162 Allied fliers including Ryherd and his two comrades.

"An ol' boy from Texas told me as we were heading east toward Germany and that we were being taken to a concentration camp," Ryherd said. "I told him he was wrong, that the Germans knew who we were and we'd surely be taken off the train in Frankfurt. Boy was I wrong."

With more than 95 souls jammed into Ryherd's car, there was not enough room to do anything but stand. The train stopped from time-to-time for toilet breaks, off-loading, and re-loading the prisoners. About the second day out, Ryherd noticed a line forming in his car. He didn't know what it was for, but figured it might be food, so he wanted his share.

"One of the Frenchmen found a loose board in the railroad car," Ryherd recalled. "It was just big enough to drop one person at a time out onto the track, so if you lie prone until the train passed, you could get up and started running."

There was just one problem with that thinking. No one knew if there was an engine "pusher" at the rear of the train. If that be the case, the cowcatcher on the front of the second locomotive would grind up anyone laying on the tracks.

"I was number 9, ready to go and take my chances," Ryherd said. "The guy ahead of me chickened out and refused to go, causing such a commotion the German guards in the next car heard us."

Seven prisoners made good their escape, one was a U.S. flier, a friend of Ryherd's. He learned later there was no "pusher" at the end of the train. "I found out later that guy made it back to England," he recalled.

The Germans were furious at losing the seven Allied prisoners. One of the guards announced that for every escapee, five would be shot the next day. Sure enough, the next day the train stopped in a country clearing, the doors were opened on Ryherd's car and one of the guards shouted "35 of you get out!"

Ryherd was near the entrance of the car and was forced out with the other 34.

"I can tell you there were no atheists among us on that day," he chuckled. "Everyone, except one, was saying their prayers. And the one who wasn't was reading his New Testament."

Just then a group of German officers walked up to inquire what was going on. After a quick huddle, the guards ordered the 35 back into the rail car.

"You never saw 35 people move that fast," he said.

Earlier, the 35, including Ryherd, had been ordered to take off every stitch of clothing. Even though it was August and hot during the day, the nights were quite cold, he recalled. The 35 huddled together trying to draw warmth from each other.

While stopped in a town just past the German border, a shot rang out. One of the guards had fired into Ryherd's car. The shot had hit one of the prisoners in the hand. It wasn't clear whether he was a Frenchman or Allied flier, but the Germans took him off the train and shot him in the back of the head and twice in the chest.

"They (Germans) were proving to us they meant business," Ryherd said. "When we got to Frankfurt, they gave us back our clothes."

After five days of standing in the cramped rail cars, the train arrived at Buchenwald Concentration Camp with the 3,000 some prisoners on Aug 21, 1944. Buchenwald is located south and east of Berlin about 50 miles. It was one of the earliest of death camps established by Hitler.

"The first thing the Germans did when we arrived was group us into five columns at 10 people deep," Ryherd recalled. "Next, we were herded over to an area where Russian prisoners of war were shaving every hair on every new prisoner's body, head-to-toe. From there we walked down into a cattle dip-affair for delousing."

(The Soviet Union was not a signer of the Geneva Convention, hence Russian military personnel, when captured, were treated differently than other Allied POWs by being placed in the death camps).

The prisoners were given khaki jackets and pants, but no cap and no shoes.

Because the concentration camp was not designed for prisoners of war, it was built adjacent to a German ammunition factory, a big target which the Royal Air Force frequently found on its nightly bombing raids.

"We were called out frequently to fight fires after the bombing, and we were barefoot," Ryherd said. "One of our guys made some shoes from a couple of pieces of wood, but a German guard saw him and nearly beat him to death with a large wooden stick."

A few days after they arrived in Buchenwald, the 162 Allied fliers were moved into a large barracks where some 250 or more young gypsy children aged 8 to 13 years were being kept.

"They were mean little guys," Ryherd recalled. "They'd steal anything worth stealing, just to survive."

Ryherd learned later the Germans loaded the children onto two railroad cars where they were gassed.

"I saw that myself," he said. "I later learned one little guy escaped and ended up being educated in this country."

Ryherd said the organization of the camp was fascinating. The German military guards were around the perimeter of the compound, but German civilian prisoners (not Jews) actually ran the camp inside. Jews were being gassed by day while the crematorium furnaces raged at night. But, not everyone who was murdered was gassed. A group of British Secret Service agents, who had been captured behind enemy lines working with the French, were ceremoniously hung in front of all the prisoners during the evening roll call. The Geneva Convention rules didn't apply to them either.

"The German civilians running the inside of the camp realized who we were and kept us Americans out of going on the work details," he recalled.

How the 162 prisoners got out of the death camp isn't quite clear, but one of the most commonly told stories has a Russian prisoner on a work detail informing the Luftwaffe (German Air Force) commandant at a nearby airfield about the Allied fliers who were being held at Buchenwald. The Luftwaffe commandant reportedly went to the camp and demanded the fliers be turned over to him. When the S.S. commandant refused, the Luftwaffe commandant informed the other than he was a personal friend of Reich Marshal Hermann Goering, and that the second-ranked Nazi behind Hitler would not want Allied prisoners mistreated. The next day, all but one of the Allied fliers were turned over to the Luftwaffe and headed for Stalag Luft III. The flier left behind was in the camp hospital and reportedly died.

"Word on the grapevine was that we were less than 24-hours from being executed," Ryherd said. "When we were interviewed by the S.S. right before our release from Buchenwald, we thought that was it. The next day, (Oct. 21, 1944), we were loaded onto trucks and taken to a train station."

Stalag Luft III was where the famous "Great Escape" was attempted earlier that same year. Ryherd was housed in the RAF section of the compound on the north side.

Although they did not know each other, there were two downed Allied fliers who eventually ended up living in North San Diego County, California. They both were on forced march in the bitter winter cold from Luft III to Nuremberg in January 1945. One of them was Ryherd, the other was John "Jack" Kellogg, now of Vista.

Second Lt. Jack Kellogg, a co-pilot, had been shot down and captured during a B-17 bombing run out of Italy over Hungary. His story is in the next chapter.

After several weeks in Nuremberg, a city under constant Allied bombing attacks, the Allied POWs were moved on to Mooseburg near Munich in southern Germany. It was in Mooseburg that General Patton's Third Army finally caught up with Ryherd and Kellogg for their rescue.

"When I saw him (Patton) come riding up in his Jeep, I thought he was the second coming....Jesus Christ himself," Ryherd laughed. "He gave a short speech and even apologized for being late."

58 THE PORT CHICAGO
DISASTER & MUTINY

One of the greatest single catastrophes during World War II did not occur on any battlefield, but alongside a dock in Northern California. The July 17, 1944 disaster at Port Chicago Naval Magazine killed 320 sailors and civilians, with another 390 injured and maimed.

The incident caused a racial controversy because most of those killed or injured were African-American sailors acting as stevedores loading munitions headed for the Pacific. At the heart of the controversy was a charge of "unsafe" loading and handling procedures by the Navy. With no procedural changes, a month after the disaster, hundreds of black sailors refused to continue loading. Many Court Martial proceedings ensued convicting the "Port Chicago 50" African-American sailors. The media dubbed it the "Port Chicago Mutiny."

The town of Port Chicago, which no longer exists, was located just north of Concord on the south shore of Suisun Bay in the estuary of the Sacramento and San Joaquin rivers. Munitions being loaded included bombs, artillery shells, naval mines, torpedoes, and small-arm ammunition. Munitions came by rail from all across the United States. Each piece was unloaded by hand from rail cars and put onto cargo ships.

Enlisted men who were assigned to the dangerous task were all black with white officers. To add to the controversy, the young sailors, who had trained at the Great Lakes Naval Training Center, were assigned to Port Chicago as stevedores with no safety training for the work.

The top scoring 30 percentage of boot camp graduates were selected to go to the fleet; the remaining low-scoring sailors were sent to Port Chicago to do the labor-intensive work. Black sailors assigned to Port Chicago were considered by their officers to be "unreliable," "emotional," lacking the ability to understand and remember orders.

Leading the recruits were black petty officers, who later were described as being "slave drivers," and "Uncle Toms." Many of the white officers were newcomers to the Navy with little or no training in supervising enlisted men, although the Navy considered them adequate for job.

Officers managed 100-man crews. They created competition by waging which crew could load the most tonnage in the shortest period of time. With no safety control, it was a recipe for disaster.

On July 13, 1944, the USS Bryan docked with 5,292 barrels of heavy fuel for the trip across the Pacific. After four days of round-the-clock loading, the ship was nearly 40 percent loaded. At 10:18 pm. on July 17, witnesses later reported a loading boom crashed to the dock, igniting an explosive. UC Berkeley reported two shock waves measuring 3.4 on the Richter scale.

Of the 320 dead personnel, only 50 could be identified. After the convictions of the "Port Chicago 50," because of public pressure, the Navy reconvened the court-martial board. The board reaffirmed the convictions, however by January 1946, some 47 of the 50 were freed, with the remaining three released several months later.

One of the results coming out of the Port Chicago

disaster/mutiny was the Navy's "desegregation" of the fleet.

This is a mere highlight of the entire story. It is complex with many factors involved. It's one of the obscure stories of World War II that seldom discussed.

59 A MOST DANGEROUS MAN

He is best-remembered as Scarlet O'Hara's unrequited love, and the illusive Scarlet Pimpernel, but to Nazi Germany's Joseph Goebbels, he was "a most dangerous man." Leslie Howard was like no other movie star.

Howard was an English-born stage and screen actor, director-producer, who starred in some of our best-known films: "Berkeley Square" (1933), "Of Human Bondage" (1934), "The Scarlet Pimpernel" (1934), "The Petrified Forest" (1936), "Pygmalion" (1938), "Intermezzo" (1939), "Gone With The Wind" (1939), "Pimpernel Smith" (1941), and "The First of the Few (1942).

What is not so well known was his production of anti-Nazi propaganda films, as well as, his alleged involvement with British Intelligence, which probably led to his death.

He was born Leslie Howard Steiner in 1893, to a British Christian mother and a Hungarian Jewish father. During World War I, the family changed their name to "Stainer," a less German-sounding moniker. During the War Howard served as a British Army officer, but suffered shell shock and was discharged in 1916.

His son, Ronald Howard (1918–1996), became an actor and was noted for portraying the title character in the 1954 BBC television series, "Sherlock Holmes."

Widely known as a ladies' man, Howard once described his amorous adventures thusly: "I didn't chase women, but I couldn't always be bothered to run away."

Howard died in 1943 on a flight from Bristol, England to Lisbon, Portugal. According to German documents, the KLM/BOAC airliner was shot down near German-occupied Bordeaux, France. Reportedly, the German pilots were angry at their squadron commander for not informing the DC-3 was a civilian aircraft.

They said they could easily have escorted the DC-3 to Bordeaux. The pilots photographed the wreckage in the Bay of Biscay, and after the war, the photographs were sent to the Howard's family.

The back-story version: the Germans believed Prime Minister Winston Churchill was on board. Later, Churchill expressed sorrow that mistake might have cost Howard his life. Churchill's bodyguard later wrote Churchill, at times, seemed clairvoyant, and, acting on a premonition, changed his departure to the following day.

Speculation by historians also have centered on whether British code-breakers had decrypted top-secret Enigma messages outlining the assassination plan, and Churchill may have wanted to protect the code-breaking operation so the Germans wouldn't suspect their Enigma machines had been compromised.

His son, Ronald, investigated the German orders in great detail, as well as British communiqués verifying intelligence reports indicating a deliberate attack on his father's plane. He speculated the Germans were aware of Churchill's real whereabouts and were not so naive as to believe the PM would be traveling alone, unescorted on an unarmed civilian aircraft.

Ronald was convinced the order to shoot down the airliner came directly from Joseph Goebbels, Nazi Minister of Propaganda. One of Leslie Howard's films ridiculed the Nazi. Goebbels believed

Howard to be "a most dangerous British propagandist."

In novelist William Stevenson's "A Man Called Intrepid," he speculated the Germans knew of Howard's mission and ordered the aircraft shot down. Stephenson further claimed Churchill knew of the German plan, but allowed it to proceed to protect the fact that the British had broken the German Enigma code.

CIA agent Joseph B. Smith recalled that, in 1957, he was briefed by the National Security Agency on Leslie Howard's death. The NSA claimed Howard knew his aircraft was to be attacked by German fighters and sacrificed himself to protect the British code-breakers.

Whatever is true, Leslie Howard was one helluva patriot and actor.

Want more World War II stories? Check out my WWII novel, "Nebraska Doppelganger" at www.tomorrowsnovels.com

60 THE BATTLE OF THE BULGE

For the armchair history buff, in a nutshell, here's the last epic European battle during World War II, which has become known as "The Battle of the Bulge."

German Dictator <u>Adolf Hitler</u> ordered an attack across the Western Front of Belgium. His goal was to compel the United States and Britain to sue for peace, freeing Germany forces to fight against the Soviets on the <u>Eastern</u> Front.

Hitler wanted to capture of the port of Antwerp, depriving the Allies of supplies.

Hitler's generals cautioned his plan was too ambitious. Nonetheless, the dictator ordered an all-out attack. The 6th SS Panzer Army would head for Antwerp. The German 5th Panzer Army, and German 7th Army would take Brussels. It would be the war's largest movement of forces against the unsuspecting Allied forces.

The Germans observed strict radio silence. Due to a low supply of fuel, one of the key elements of the attack was to capture Allied gasoline depots. Allied bombardment of the Rumanian oil fields left the Germans desperately low; without the fuel depots, their tanks had little chance in reaching Antwerp.

A special German unit was formed to infiltrate Allied lines dressed as American soldiers and spread confusion. Road signs were switched, and Germans posing as G.I. Military Police confused traffic flow. Allied Supreme Commander General Dwight D. "Ike" Eisenhower was completely unaware.

At 5:30 am. on December 16, 1944, the German offensive began on the 6th Panzer Army's front. Meeting heavy resistance from the Americans, the Germans were forced to commit tanks to the battle. In the center, German troops opened a gap through the U.S. 28th and 106th Infantry Divisions, capturing two U.S. regiments in the process, creating a huge bulge in the front line.

The 5th Panzer Army's advance was slowed allowing the U.S. 101st Airborne to reach the vital crossroads at Bastogne. With snowstorms in one of the bitterly coldest winters on record, it prevented Allied air power from support. In the south, the German infantry was essentially stopped by the U.S. VIII Corps.

Later that first day, members of a SS Waffen Panzer battalion captured and executed some 150 Americans in a field near Malmedy. This action became infamously known as "The Malmedy Massacre".

Encountering heavy resistance at Stoumont, Belgium, the Germans ran out of fuel and were forced to abandon their vehicles.

American troops fought a critical action at St. Vith, but they were soon driven back by the Germans. This collapse caused the U.S. 101st Airborne and the U.S. 10th Armored Division's Combat Command B at Bastogne to be surrounded.

At Bastogne, the Americans repelled numerous German assaults while fighting in bitter cold weather. Short on supplies and ammunition, the U.S. 101st's commander, Brig. General Anthony McAuliffe rebuffed a German demand for surrender by replying, "Nuts!"

Ike asked how long it would take for Lt. General George Patton's Third Army to advance north. Patton replied: "48 hours." No one believed him, but he did it and rescued the encircled

American troops.

On Dec. 24, with clear weather, Allied fighter-bombers entered the battle. That same day, more German forces ran out of fuel and stopped 10 miles short of the Meuse River.

German commanders urged Hitler to halt the attack, but he angrily refused. Soon after, the German forces ground to a halt – literally out of gas. The Western Front returned to the Dec. 16 positions.

During the Battle of the Bulge, 20,876 Allied soldiers were killed, with 42,893 wounded and 23,554 captured or missing. German losses: 15,652 killed, 41,600 wounded, and 27,582 captured or missing.

Defeated in the campaign, German offensive capability in the West was destroyed. The Battle of the Bulge has gone down as one of the largest and deadliest and futile encounters in modern warfare.

61 THE MALMEDY MASSACRE

In the bitter-cold winter of 1944, the Allied forces were racing to the Rhine River to overthrow the German Nazi regime; at the same time, the enemy was desperately trying to break through and recapture the port at Antwerp, Belgium. During what became known as "The Battle of the Bulge," several atrocities took place on both sides, but most of those by the Allies were in retaliation against the murders of POWs and civilians committed by the Nazi Waffen SS.

The "Malmedy Massacre" was a heinous-crime where 84 U.S. POWs were murdered by their German captors near Malmedy, Belgium. The atrocity was committed on December 17, 1944, by members of Colonel Joachim Peiper's SS panzer command.

In order to frighten the Allied troops, Hitler ordered the last-ditch counter-offensive to be carried out with a brutality previously used by the Nazis on the Eastern Front in Russia. During his 1946 war-crimes trial in Dachau, Peiper testified "… no quarter was to be granted, no prisoners taken, and no pity shown towards Belgian civilians.

The German SS unit approached the Malmedy crossroads as an American convoy of about 30 trucks and Jeeps arrived. Peiper's troops opened fire on the American convoy, immobilizing the first and last vehicles of the column, forcing it to halt. Armed with only rifles and other small arms, the Americans had to surrender to the Nazi heavily-armed tank force.

While Peiper's column continued to move on, a contingent of SS troops left behind, took the American prisoners to a nearby field and opened fire with machine guns. The Americans panicked. Some tried to flee, but most were shot where they stood. A few sought shelter in a café at the crossroads, but SS troops set fire to the building, and shot all who tried to escape the flames. Some in the field had dropped to the ground and pretended to be dead when the shooting began. However, SS troops walked among the bodies and shot any who appeared to be alive.

By late evening of December 17, rumors Nazis were killing POWs had reached American forces. One unit promptly issued orders that "No SS troops or paratroopers will be taken prisoner but will be shot on sight." There are claims some of the American forces retaliated by killing German prisoners at what became known as the "Chenogne Massacre."

The size of the Malmedy Massacre caused unusual attention and protest because it was the only one perpetrated on such a large scale against American troops by the Germans during the war. For Malmedy, the Dachau war crimes tribunal tried more than 70 SS soldiers and pronounced 43 death sentences (none of which were ever carried out) and 22 life sentences. Eight other men were sentenced to shorter prison sentences.

All the convicted were released during the 1950s, the last one to leave prison was Peiper in December 1956.

Peiper lived in France following his prison release. In 1974, a former Communist resistance fighter uncovered the former SS colonel's presence in France. Peiper sent his family back to Germany, but he stayed behind. During the night of July 13, 1976, a gunfight took place at Peiper's house, which was set on fire.

Peiper's charred body was found the next day with a bullet in his chest. He had just started writing a book about Malmedy and what action followed. Peiper's attackers were never identified.

62 THE GENERAL BEHIND THE GENERALS

One of the most important figures during the war-torn mid-20th century was General George C. Marshall.

Marshall, born Dec. 31, 1880, was an American soldier and statesman famous for his leadership roles during World War II and the Korean War. He was Chief of Staff of the U.S. Army, Secretary of State, and Secretary of Defense.

In 1917, during the First World War, Marshall was posted to American Expeditionary Forces headquarters where he worked closely with his mentor, General John J. Pershing, and was a key planner of American operations instrumental to the defeat of Germany.

Brigadier General Marshall was assigned to the War Plans Division in Washington D.C. and subsequently reassigned as Deputy Chief of Staff.

In 1939, President Roosevelt proposed a plan to provide aircraft to England. Everyone supported the idea except Marshall. The general belief was Marshall had just ended his career, but his opposing view impressed Roosevelt, who nominated him to be Army Chief of Staff. Marshall was promoted to General and sworn in on September 1, 1939, the day German forces invaded

Poland.

Marshall organized the largest military expansion in United States history, inheriting an outmoded, poorly equipped army of 189,000 men. Though he had never actually led troops in combat, Marshall was a skilled organizer with a talent for inspiring other officers. Most of the prominent American generals who were key to victory in Europe such as Dwight Eisenhower, George Patton, Omar Bradley, and Mark Clark, were selected by Marshall.

Faced with the necessity of turning an army of former civilians into a potent force by 1942, Marshall directed efforts on quickly producing 8 million soldiers. At the time, most U.S. commanders at lower levels had little, or no combat experience of any kind. As a result, Army forces deploying to Africa suffered serious defeats when encountering German Field Marshall Erwin Rommel's armored combat units in Africa at Kasserine Pass and other major battles.

Marshall wrote the document that would become the central strategy for all Allied operations in Europe. It was assumed Marshall would become the Supreme Commander of Operation Overlord (D-day), but Roosevelt selected Eisenhower. Roosevelt didn't want to lose Marshall's presence. He told Marshall, "I didn't feel I could sleep at ease if you were out of Washington."

On December 16, 1944, Marshall became the first American General to be promoted to five-star rank, the newly created General of the Army – the American equivalent rank to Field Marshal. William Leahy had been promoted to U.S. Navy Fleet Admiral the previous day.

In early 1947, Truman appointed Marshall Secretary of State. He became the spokesman for the State Department's ambitious plans to rebuild Europe. Rebuilding various war-torn countries was designed primarily by the State Department. The plan's success resulted in Marshall received the Nobel Peace Prize in 1953 for what became known as the "Marshall Plan."

Marshall strongly opposed recognizing the state of Israel. He said if Israel was recognized a war would break out. In 1948, war erupted -- one day after Israel's declaration.

In 1950, the opening months of the Korean War revealed a poorly prepared military, so Truman named Marshall Secretary of Defense. He finally retired for good a year later. Marshall died at 78 on Oct. 16, 1959.

Truman once declared, "I don't think...there has been a man who has been a greater administrator or with a knowledge of military affairs equal to General Marshall."

63 PATTON: AN AMERICAN FOLK HERO

George Smith Patton, Jr. (November 11, 1885 – December 21, 1945) was a United States Army general, best known for his command of the Seventh United States Army, and later the Third United States Army, in the European Theater of World War II.

Born in 1885 to a privileged family with an extensive military background, Patton attended the Virginia Military Institute, and later the U.S. Military Academy at West Point. He participated in the 1912 Olympic Modern Pentathlon, and was instrumental in designing the M1913 "Patton Saber". Patton first saw combat during the Pancho Villa Expedition in 1916, taking part in America's first military action using motor vehicles. He later joined the newly formed United States Tank Corps of the American Expeditionary Forces and saw action in World War I, first commanding the U.S. Tank School in France before being wounded near the end of the war. In the interwar period, Patton remained a central figure in the development of armored warfare doctrine in the U.S. Army, serving on numerous staff positions throughout the country. Rising through the ranks, he commanded the U.S. 2nd Armored Division at the time of the U.S. entry into World War II.

Patton led U.S. troops into the Mediterranean theater with an invasion of Casablanca during Operation Torch in 1942, where he later established himself as an effective commander through his rapid rehabilitation of the demoralized U.S. II Corps.

He commanded the Seventh Army during the Invasion of Sicily, where he was the first Allied Commander to reach Messina. There he was embroiled in controversy after he slapped two shell-shocked soldiers under his command, and was temporarily removed from battlefield command for other duties such as participating in Operation Fortitude's Disinformation campaign for Operation Overlord.

Patton returned to command the Third Army following the invasion of Normandy in 1944, where he led a highly successful, rapid-armored drive across France. He led the relief of beleaguered U.S. troops at Bastogne during the Battle of the Bulge, and advanced his army into Nazi Germany by the end of the war.

After the war, Patton became the Military Governor of Bavaria, but he was relieved of this post because of his statements on denazification. He commanded the Fifteenth United States Army for slightly more than two months. Patton died following an automobile accident in Europe on December 21, 1945.

Patton's colorful image, hard-driving personality and success as a commander were at times overshadowed by his controversial public statements regarding the Soviet Union, which were out of accord with American foreign policy. But his philosophy of leading from the front, and his ability to inspire his troops with vulgarity-ridden speeches, such as a famous address to the Third Army, attracted favorable attention. His strong emphasis on rapid and aggressive offensive action proved effective. While Allied leaders held sharply differing opinions on Patton, he was regarded highly by his opponents in the German High Command. A popular, award-winning biographical film released in 1970 helped transform Patton into an American folk hero.

64 EDDIE ALBERT – AN UNSUNG HERO

Edward Albert Heimberger had a very long resume that included being a businessman, insurance salesman, nightclub singer, circus performer, Army intelligence agent, pioneer television star, Hollywood character actor, environmental activist, and World War II decorated Naval hero.

Better known in TV and movies audiences as Eddie Albert, he was born April 22, 1906, in Rock Island, Illinois. He was nominated twice for Best Supporting Actor (Roman Holiday, 1954; The Heartbreak Kid, 1973), and appeared in some 90 television productions. Among his many top film performances include "Brother Rat," "Oklahoma," "Captain Newman, M.D."and "The Longest Yard."

Prior to the War, Albert had toured Mexico working as a clown and high-wire artist with a Circus, but secretly, he worked for U.S. Army intelligence, photographing German U-boats moored in Mexican harbors.

On Sept. 9, 1942, Albert enlisted in the United States Navy and became an officer. He was awarded the Bronze Star with Combat "V" for his heroism during the 1943 invasion of Tarawa. As commander of a landing craft, Albert, under heavy enemy fire, rescued 77 <u>Marines</u> stranded offshore.

As a teenager, he went to Central High School in Minneapolis and joined the drama club with schoolmate Harriette Lake (later known as actress <u>Ann Sothern</u>). They graduated in the class of 1926. Then Albert entered the <u>University of Minnesota</u>, where he majored in business. After graduation, he embarked on a business career, but the <u>stock market crash in 1929</u>, left him unemployed. Albert stopped using his last name since it invariably was mispronounced as "Hamburger." He moved to <u>New York City</u> in 1933, where he co-hosted a radio show. After the show's three-year run, Albert was offered a film contract by <u>Warner Bros.</u>

Eddie Albert became one of the earliest television actors, performing live in one of <u>RCA</u>'s first television broadcasts. Albert wrote and performed in the very first <u>teleplay</u>, The Love Nest, which was aired "live" on November 6, 1936.

In 1938, he made his <u>feature film</u> debut in the <u>Hollywood</u> version of "<u>Brother Rat</u>" with <u>Ronald Reagan</u> and <u>Jane Wyman</u>, reprising his Broadway role of "Bing" Edwards. Then, he starred in "<u>On Your Toes</u>." Back on Broadway he did hit shows such as "<u>The Seven Year Itch</u>" (1952–1955) and in 1960 Albert replaced <u>Robert Preston</u> in "<u>The Music Man</u>."

In 1965, Albert starred in "<u>Green Acres</u>," co-starring <u>Eva Gabor</u> as his urbanite, spoiled wife. The show was an immediate hit. Then, in 1975, Albert starred in the popular <u>crime drama</u> "<u>Switch</u>" as a retired police officer, Frank McBride, who goes to work as a private detective.

In his personal life, Albert married Mexican actress <u>Margo</u> María Castilla in 1945. They had a son, <u>Edward Jr.</u>, in 1951, who also became an actor. They adopted a daughter, Maria, who became her father's business manager. Margo Albert died from <u>brain cancer</u> in 1980.

In his final years, Albert suffered from Alzheimer's. Edward Jr., put his acting career on hold to care for his father. Albert senior died of <u>pneumonia</u> in 2005 at the age of 99. He is interred at <u>Westwood Village Memorial Park Cemetery</u>, next to his late wife, and close to his Green Acres co-star <u>Eva Gabor</u>. Edward Jr. died a year after his father, suffering from <u>lung cancer</u>. He was 55.

65 THE MAN WHO WOULD BE BOND

Born May 28, 1908, Ian Lancaster Fleming was a famed English author, journalist and British Naval Intelligence officer, who lived many of the actual experiences he wrote about in his James Bond series of spy novels.

Fleming came from a wealthy family. His father was a member of Parliament until his death in 1917 during World War I.

While working for Britain's Naval Intelligence Division during the Second World War, Fleming was involved in planning "Operation Goldeneye" and in the planning and oversight of two intelligence units, 30 Assault Unit and T-Force. His wartime service and his career as a journalist provided much of the background, detail, and depth of his novels.

Fleming wrote his first Bond novel, *Casino Royale* in 1952. It was a success, with three print runs being commissioned to cope with the demand. Eleven Bond novels and two short-story collections followed between 1953 and 1966. The novels revolved around James Bond, an officer in the Secret Intelligence Service, commonly known as MI6. Bond was also known by his code number, 007, and was a commander in the Royal Naval Reserve. The Bond stories rank among the best-selling series of fictional books of all time, having sold over 100-million copies worldwide. Fleming also wrote the children's story *Chitty-Chitty-Bang-Bang* and two works of non-fiction. In 2008, The Times ranked Fleming 14th on its list of "The 50 greatest British writers since 1945".

He was married to Ann Charteris, who was divorced from the second Viscount Rothermere as a result of her affair with Fleming. Fleming and Charteris had a son, Caspar. Fleming was a heavy smoker and drinker who suffered from heart disease; he died in 1964, aged 56, from a heart attack. Two of his James Bond books were published posthumously; other writers have since produced Bond novels. Fleming's creation has appeared in film twenty-five times, portrayed by seven actors.

In May 1939, Fleming was recruited by Rear Admiral John Godfrey, Director of Naval Intelligence of the Royal Navy, to become his personal assistant. He joined the organization full-time in August 1939, with the codename "17-F," and worked out of Room 39 at The Admiralty.

Fleming's biographer, Andrew Lycett, notes that Fleming had "no obvious qualifications" for the role. As part of his appointment, Fleming was commissioned into the Royal Naval Volunteer Reserve in July 1939, initially as lieutenant, but promoted to commander a few months later.

Fleming proved invaluable as Godfrey's personal assistant and excelled in administration. Godfrey was known as an abrasive character who made enemies within government circles. He frequently used Fleming as a liaison with other sections of the government's wartime administration, such as the Secret Intelligence Service, the Political Warfare Executive, the Special Operations Executive (SOE), the Joint Intelligence Committee and the Prime Minister's staff.

On 29 September 1939, soon after the start of the war, Godfrey circulated a memorandum that, "bore all the hallmarks of... Lieutenant Commander Ian Fleming", according to historian Ben Macintyre. It was called the Trout Memo and compared the deception of an enemy in wartime to fly fishing. The memo contained a number of schemes to be considered for use against the Axis powers to lure U-boats and German surface ships towards minefields. Number 28 on the list was an idea to plant misleading papers on a corpse that would be found by the enemy; this suggestion is similar to Operation Mincemeat, the successful 1943 plan to conceal the intended invasion of Italy from North Africa, although that idea was developed by Charles Cholmondoley in October 1942. The recommendation in the Trout Memo was titled: "A Suggestion (not a very nice one)," and continued: "The following suggestion is used in a book by Basil Thomson: a corpse dressed as an airman, with dispatches in his pockets, could be dropped on the coast, supposedly from a parachute that has failed. I understand there is no difficulty in obtaining corpses at the Naval Hospital, but, of course, it would have to be a fresh one."

In 1940, Fleming and Godfrey contacted Kenneth Mason, Professor of Geography at Oxford University, about the preparation of reports on the geography of countries involved in military operations. These reports were the precursors of the Naval Intelligence Division Geographical Handbook Series produced between 1941 and 1946.

Operation Ruthless, a plan aimed at obtaining details of the Enigma codes used by Nazi Germany's Navy, was instigated by a memo written by Fleming to Godfrey on 12 September 1940. The idea was to "obtain" a German bomber, man it with a German-speaking crew dressed in Luftwaffe uniforms, and crash it into the English Channel. The crew would then attack their German rescuers and bring their boat and Enigma machine back to England. Much to the annoyance of Alan Turing and Peter Twinn at Bletchley Park, the mission was never carried out. According to Fleming's niece, Lucy, an official at the Royal Air Force pointed out that if they were to drop a downed Heinkel bomber in the English Channel, it would probably sink rather quickly.

Fleming also worked with Colonel "Wild Bill" Donovan,

President Franklin D. Roosevelt's special representative on intelligence co-operation between London and Washington. In May 1941, Fleming accompanied Godfrey to the United States, where he assisted in writing a blueprint for the Office of the Coordinator of Information, the department which turned into the Office of Strategic Services and eventually became the CIA.

In 1941-42, Admiral Godfrey put Fleming in charge of Operation Golden Eye, a plan to maintain an intelligence framework in Spain in the event of a German takeover of the territory. Fleming's plan involved maintaining communication with Gibraltar and launching sabotage operations against the Nazis. In 1941, Fleming liaised with Donovan over American involvement in a measure intended to ensure that the Germans did not dominate the seaways.

66 30-ASSAULT UNIT...

In 1942, Ian Lancaster Fleming formed a unit of commandos, known as No. 30 Commando or 30 Assault Unit (30-AU), composed of specialist intelligence troops.

30-AU's job was to be near the front line of an advance-sometimes in front of it—to seize enemy documents from previously targeted headquarters. The unit was based on a German group headed by Otto Skorzeny, who had undertaken similar activities in the Battle of Crete in May 1941. The German unit was thought by Fleming to be "one of the most outstanding innovations in German intelligence." Fleming did not fight in the field with the unit, but selected targets and directed operations from the rear.[40]

On its formation the unit was only thirty strong, but it grew to five times that size. The unit was filled with men from other commando units, and trained in unarmed combat, safe-cracking and lock-picking at the SOE facilities. In late 1942 Captain (later Rear-Admiral) Edmund Rushbrooke replaced Godfrey as head of the Naval Intelligence Division, and Fleming's influence in the organization declined, although he retained control over 30-AU. Fleming was unpopular with the unit's members, who disliked his referring to them as his "Red Indians."

Before the Normandy landings, most of 30AU's operations were in the Mediterranean, although it secretly participated in the Dieppe Raid in a failed pinch raid for an Enigma machine and related materials. Because of its successes in Sicily and Italy, 30AU became greatly trusted by naval intelligence. In March 1944, Fleming oversaw the distribution of intelligence to Royal Navy units in preparation for Operation Overlord and followed the unit into Germany after it located, in Tambach Castle, the German naval archives from 1870.

Fleming visited 30AU in the field during and after Operation Overlord, especially following an attack on Cherbourg for which he was concerned that the unit had been incorrectly used as a regular commando force rather than an intelligence-gathering unit. This wasted the men's specialist skills, risked their safety on operations that did not justify the use of such skilled operatives, and threatened the vital gathering of intelligence. Afterward, the management of these units was revised.[44] Fleming was replaced as head of 30AU on 6 June 1944, but maintained some involvement.[48] In December 1944, he was posted on an intelligence fact-finding trip to the Far East on behalf of the Director of Naval Intelligence. Much of the trip was spent identifying opportunities for 30-AU in the Pacific, although the unit ultimately saw little action because of the Japanese surrender.

The success of 30AU led to the August 1944 decision to establish a "Target Force", which became known as T-Force. The official memorandum, held at The National Archives in London, describes the unit's primary role: "T-Force = Target Force, to guard and secure documents, persons, equipment, with combat and Intelligence personnel, after capture of large towns, ports etc. in liberated and enemy territory."

Fleming sat on the committee that selected the targets for the T-Force unit, and listed them in the "Black Books" that were issued to the unit's officers. The infantry component of T-Force was in part made up of the 5th Battalion, King's Regiment, which supported the Second Army.[54] It was responsible for securing targets of interest for the British military, including nuclear laboratories, gas research centers and individual rocket scientists. The unit's most notable discoveries came during the advance on the German port of Kiel, in the research center for German engines used in the V-2 rocket, Messerschmitt Me 163 fighters and high-speed U-boats.[55] Fleming would later use elements of the activities of T-Force in his writing, particularly in his 1955 Bond novel Moonraker.[56]

In 1942 Fleming attended an Anglo-American intelligence summit in Jamaica and, despite the constant heavy rain during his visit, he decided to live on the island once the war was over.[57] His friend, Ivar Bryce, helped find a plot of land in Saint Mary Parish where, in 1945, Fleming had a house built, which he named Goldeneye.[58] The name of the house and estate where he wrote his novels has many possible sources. Fleming himself mentioned both his wartime Operation Golden Eye and Carson McCullers' 1941 novel Reflections in a Golden Eye, which described the use of British naval bases in the Caribbean by the American Navy.

67 HARRY S. TRUMAN: 'HIS ACCIDENTCY'

The 33rd U.S. President, Harry S. Truman, often was referred to as "His Accidentcy" by detractors. It was a mocking reference to his becoming the nation's chief executive upon the April 12, 1945, sudden death of Franklin D. Roosevelt.

Born May 8, 1884 to a Missouri farm couple, Truman was only a high school graduate, but he made some of the momentous decisions of the 20th century, including the biggest in world history: to drop the first two atomic bombs that resulted in the end of World War II.

But almost immediately in the aftermath of World War II, the United States found itself the most powerful nation in the world. Political tensions with the Soviet Union over the rebuilding of Europe increased, marking the start of the Cold War.

Truman spent most of his youth on his family's farm. During World War I, he served in combat in France as an artillery officer in his National Guard unit. After the war, he briefly owned a haberdashery and joined the Democratic Party political machine of Tom Pendergast in Kansas City, Missouri. Truman was first elected to public office as a county official and became a U.S. Senator in 1935. He gained national prominence as head of the

Truman Committee formed in March 1941, which exposed waste, fraud, and corruption in wartime contracts.

During the 1944 Democratic convention, a fight broke out over who would be nominated as Roosevelt's running mate. It was feared the President, if re-elected for a fourth term, would not live to see it through. Democrats didn't want Vice President Henry Wallace, an avowed left-leaning socialist, taking over the presidency, especially during war time. Senator Truman was a compromise and ultimately became President in only 82 days upon Roosevelt's death.

Roosevelt died less than a month before Germany surrendered, but the war in the Pacific dragged on. Truman had never been told about the ultra-secret Manhattan Project – the development of the atom bomb. When he was briefed on the enormity of the project and the potential of ending the war, the new president had a momentous decision. If the Japanese home islands had to be assaulted, an estimated one million U.S. troops could be lost, dragging the war on for another year. If the bomb was dropped, it could quickly end the war. Truman didn't mull over the decision very long. He gave the order to use the bombs. After bombing Hiroshima, Japan and Nagasaki, Japan, the Japanese surrendered unconditionally.

Following the war, Truman assisted in the founding of the United Nations, issued the Truman Doctrine in an effort to thwart communism, and passed the $13 billion Marshall Plan to rebuild Europe, including the Axis Powers of Germany, Italy, and Japan.

In 1948, as the "Cold War" began, Truman oversaw the Berlin Airlift and in 1949 the creation of North Atlantic Treaty Organization (NATO).

When communist North Korea invaded South Korea in 1950, Truman immediately sent in U.S. troops and gained UN approval for the Korean War. Probably the most unpopular decision Truman made was the firing of five-star General Douglas MacArthur, who wanted to expand the war in Korea. History has mostly vindicated Truman on a decision that possibly avoided World War III.

Popular and scholarly assessments of Truman's presidency were initially poor, but have become more positive in recent years. Truman's upset victory over New York Governor Thomas Dewey is considered one of the great victories of American politics.

On December 26, 1972, Truman at the age of 88 died. His wife, Bess, opted for a private burial service for her husband at the Truman Library in Independence, Missouri, rather than a state funeral in Washington.

68 WHEN 'FATHER' WAS IN WASHINGTON, D.C.

During most of the '50s, Dwight David Eisenhower was President and because of his historic guidance that won the war in Europe, many looked upon "Ike" as a father-figure.

Born Oct. 4, 1890, and raised in Abilene, Kansas, Eisenhower was the typical "All-American" boy. He excelled at the U.S. Military Academy (West Point), graduating in a class that would be tagged, "The class the stars fell upon." No less than a dozen classmates of Ike's went on to play significant roles as generals in World War II. Ike would end up as Supreme Allied Commander in Europe, leading the Allied forces to victory over Germany and Italy.

While he appeared to be a mild-mannered soldier, Ike was anything but...He began being noticed during the 1930s when he served as General Douglas MacArthur's Chief of Staff in Washington, D.C., and later in the Philippines. Ike was assigned to Army headquarters in Washington, D.C. by General George Marshall, Army Chief of Staff.

After the attack on Pearl Harbor on December 7, 1941, Marshall elevated him in rank over more senior officers.

In 1942, Ike was put in command of Operation Torch, where American troops joined British forces to oust Germany from North Africa. He soon was elevated to the war-time rank of five-star General and was made Supreme Commander of the Allied Forces in Europe. Ike was responsible for planning and supervising the June 6, 1944 invasion (D-Day), which was the largest military assault in modern history. Because of it, on May 8, 1945, Germany surrendered.

After the Japanese surrendered three months later, in August 1945, President Truman appointed Ike as Army Chief of Staff and later as the first Supreme Commander of the newly-formed North Atlantic Treaty Organization (NATO).

In 1952, both the Democrats and Republicans wooed Ike to run for President, but no one was sure which party he favored. Ike won election in a landslide as a Republican.

President Eisenhower's main goals were to keep pressure on the Soviet Union and reduce federal deficits. Ike was not a good speaker, but there was no doubt as to who was in charge. He was the epitome of a world leader.

In the first year of his presidency, Ike threatened the use of nuclear weapons in order to conclude the Korean War. His policy of nuclear deterrence prioritized inexpensive nuclear weapons. In 1954, Eisenhower rejected sending U.S. military force to help the French retain their colony of Vietnam.

In 1957, after the Soviet Union launched the world's first artificial satellite, Ike authorized the establishment of National Aeronautics & Space Agency (NASA), which ignited the space race. During the Suez Crisis of 1956, Eisenhower condemned the Israel, British, and French invasion of Egypt, and forced them to withdraw.

Taking a lesson from Germany's modern autobahn, Ike launched the Interstate Highway System. Interestingly enough, he started the Defense Advanced Research Projects Agency (which led to the Internet). He also established a strong science education program and encouraged the peaceful use of nuclear power.

In 1956, Ike ordered the federal court to desegregate public schools. He also signed civil rights legislation in 1957 and 1960 to protect the right to vote. During his tenure, Ike made five appointments to the U.S. Supreme Court.

In his farewell address to the nation, Eisenhower expressed his concerns about the dangers of corporate control of Congress and massive military spending, particularly deficit spending, and government contracts to private military manufacturers, and coined the term "Military-Industrial-Congressional Complex." Future presidents wouldn't heed the warning.

Voted Gallup's most admired man 12 times, Ike achieved widespread popular esteem both in and out of office. His two terms saw economic prosperity across the nation. Since the late 20th century, consensus among Western scholars has consistently held Eisenhower to be one of our greatest Presidents.

69 THE ROSENBERG: SPIES OR POLITICAL DUPES?

One of the most controversial episodes in American history was the capture, trial, and execution of Ethel and Julius Rosenberg.

The couple were American citizens executed on June 19, 1953, for conspiracy to commit espionage. They were accused and convicted of espionage and passing atomic bomb secrets to the Soviet Union. What makes the case controversial is all others convicted of passing secrets, received varying lengths of prison sentences.

The question remains: Why were just the Rosenbergs executed?

In 1995, after the collapse of the Soviet Union, the United States government released a series of decoded Soviets cables confirming that Julius acted as a courier and recruiter for the Russians. The documents were ambiguous about Ethel's involvement. Other spies connected with the case, who were captured by the FBI, included: David Greenglass, (Ethel's brother), Harry Gold, and German scientist Klaus Fuchs. Greenglass supplied documents to Julius from Los Alamos, New Mexico. He served 10 years of a 15-year sentence. Harry Gold, who identified Klaus Fuchs, served 15 years for being the courier for Greenglass.

Morton Sobell, who was tried along with the Rosenbergs, served a 17 years of a 30-year sentence. In 2008, Sobell admitted he was a spy and confirmed that Julius, indeed, provided classified atomic information to the Soviets.

Perhaps the most incredible of the sentences went to German scientist Klaus Fuchs, who served only nine years. The nuclear scientist was convicted of passing secrets to the Soviets from A-bomb research facilities in England.

Julius went to work for the United States Army Signal Corps' engineering research laboratories at Fort Monmouth, New Jersey, in 1940. He worked as an engineer-inspector until 1945, when he was fired after the Army discovered he was a member of the Communist Party.

Julius Rosenberg was originally recruited by the Soviet secret police in 1942. According to his former handler, Alexandre Feklisov, Julius provided thousands of Top-Secret documents including missile plans of which an upgraded model was used in 1960 to shoot down Gary Powers' U-2 spy plane.

Among the most damning information in the Soviet cables named Julius Rosenberg as the head of the A-bomb spy ring. While this fact wasn't proven during the trial, Feklisov's confirmation a half-century later quells those who said the Rosenbergs were dupes.

According to Feklisov in recent years, Julius was responsible for passing a complete set of design and production drawings for Lockheed's P-80 "Shooting Star" fighter planes, the first operational jet in the U.S. Air Force.

Julius and Ethel Rosenberg were the only two American civilians to be executed for espionage during the Cold War. The judge held them responsible not only for espionage, but also for the 50,000 U.S. deaths of the Korean War.

The Rosenbergs were held up as examples of "scapegoats' by those against their convictions. The "Red Scare" dominated the next four decades of American life. When it came time to carry out the sentences, the federal government did not have an electric chair, so the one at New York state's Sing-Sing prison was used. Adding to the controversy was the execution itself. Eyewitness testimony said Julius died immediately from required series of three electric jolts, but Ethel was still alive, requiring two more jolts before she was declared dead.

The Rosenbergs' two sons spent years trying to prove the innocence of their parents, but after Morton Sobel confessed to the affair in 2008, the sons acknowledged their father had been involved in espionage, but maintained their parents were not involved in passing A-bomb secrets.

70 THE FOUNDING OF AMERICA'S NEW PASTIME

With the annual Super Bowl Sunday just around the corner, you might be interested in how professional football grew to the giant business it is today.

Baseball is no longer the nation's "pastime." Today, it's the *National Football League*. The NFL averages a larger per-game viewership, both in attendance, as well as, broadcasts and telecasts, than any other sporting event in North America.

On February 1, this year's ultimate playoff, known as the "Super Bowl," will determine the champion of the league.

Professional football had its birth in the state of Ohio when a meeting in a new-car showroom was held on August 20, 1920, by representatives of the *Akron Pros, Canton Bulldogs, Cleveland Indians*, and *Dayton Triangles* in Canton, Ohio, resulting in the formation of the *"American Professional Football Conference."* The primary aim was to raise the standard of professional football, eliminating bidding for players between clubs and to organize schedules.

The fledgling league hired legendary football great Jim Thorpe as the first president. Historically speaking, only two of those original 14 teams remain: the *Decatur Staleys* (now the *Chicago Bears*) and the *Chicago Cardinals* (now the *Arizona Cardinals*).

In 1922, the name was changed to the *National Football League*. Fan interest in a championship game led the NFL to split into two divisions with a championship game to be played between the divisions. In the 1933 season, African Americans were prohibited from playing in the league. That ban was rescinded in 1947, because of public pressure and the lifting of a similar ban in Major League Baseball.

Up until the 1960s, several smaller leagues attempted to form, but the NFL remained dominant and faced little competition. Rival leagues included three attempts at an, *"American Football League,"* the *"World Football League,* and the *"All-America Football Conference,"* none of which lasted for more than four seasons; although, several of the teams joined the NFL after their parent league disbanded.

A fourth attempt at an *"American Football League,"* began in 1960. The upstart AFL challenged the established NFL, gaining lucrative television contracts and a bidding war for free agents and draft picks. In 1966, the two leagues finally announced a merger to take full effect in 1970.

In 1966, the leagues began holding a common draft and championship game, the Super Bowl. The four championship games before the merger saw the NFL winning the first two, and the AFL won Super Bowl III and Super Bowl IV. After the league merged, two conferences were formed: the NFC and the AFC.

In 1967, the NFL expanded to 16 teams. Instead of just evening out the conferences by adding the expansion *New Orleans Saints*, the NFL realigned the conferences, and split each into two four-team divisions. The four conference champions would meet for a two-round playoff.

Today, much of the NFL's growth is attributed to the late Pete Rozelle, who led the league from 1960 to 1989. Overall annual attendance increased from 3 million at the beginning of Rozelle's tenure as commissioner to 17 million by his retirement. Success can be measured in the numbers. On February 1, nearly a billion TV viewers around-the-world are expected to be watching the Super Bowl. A sell-out crowd will watch the game in person, paying several hundred dollars for a ticket.

Aside from the games, in 1983, Rozelle established NFL Properties, earning the league billions of dollars annually in jerseys, sweatshirts, shirts, caps, etc., sales. The NFL is an enormously wealthy business for its owners and players.

ABOUT THE AUTHOR

The author is a 40 year is an award-winning veteran of journalism in newspapers, magazines, radio, and television. He has written eight books, four of them historical novels. He graduated from Phoenix College and Arizona State University studying Journalism and history.

Morrow was a columnist, feature writer, editor and publisher for several weekly and daily newspapers in Oregon, Arizona, and Southern California. He spent 10 years in public relations, first as vice president for communications and historian for the world-famous Hotel del Coronado, then co-owner of a public relations and advertising agency in San Diego.

The last 20 years of his newspaper career were spent in Oceanside, California as a daily columnist for the daily Blade-Citizen, which later became the North County Times.

Today, Morrow writes a weekly history column for local weekly newspaper. He has written four of his novels which were published before this latest tome.

Please visit my website: www.getmorrowsnovels.com

Made in the USA
Columbia, SC
24 September 2019